ARABIC THOUGHT
AND THE WESTERN WORLD

ARABIC THOUGHT
AND THE
WESTERN WORLD
in the Golden Age of Islam

EUGENE A. MYERS
Pennsylvania State University

FREDERICK UNGAR PUBLISHING CO.
NEW YORK

CONTENTS

INTRODUCTION

Islam was born midway in the first half of the seventh century A.D. Military victories came surprisingly fast to the Arabic believers. Syria, Iraq, Persia, Egypt were early victims. In A.D. 711 the Iberian Peninsula was conquered; but in 732, after capturing several towns in Gaul, the Arab army was checked between Tours and Poitiers by Charles Martel. In any event, it took only one hundred years for the followers of Islam to become masters of an empire extending from the Bay of Biscay to the Indus and the confines of China and from the Aral Sea to the lower cataracts of the Nile.

Religious activities kept pace with military victories; conversion matched territorial conquests. The Ibadite sect, representing the simplicity of primitive Islamic theology, law, and politics, was founded, and also the orthodox schools of Moslem law—the Hanafite (early in the eighth century) and the Malikite (second half of the eighth century). Malik, founder of the school named for him, at that time compiled the earliest collection of traditional beliefs. It is generally agreed that few people have taken their religion more seriously than did the early Moslems; this fervor was evidently the main cause of their cohesion and their strength against enemies who were divided and whose faith was by comparison tepid and weak.

Despite military victories and an aggressive new religion, Islamic culture and science lagged. One might think that temporal and spiritual triumph would spur on a nation to bid for leadership in every field. However, Islam did not take its place

7

at the center of world learning until knowledge accumulated by other peoples had been translated into Arabic.

Translation, then, is proved here to be of paramount importance. Translation enables one culture to learn from others, and its enriching results are often greater than the sum of the parts. Prior to A.D. 750 very few works were translated into Arabic from any other language, and the Arabs had very little to boast of except military victories. But Western science and culture were also at a low ebb while Moslem science had not yet begun. Stirring influences, however, were already at work.

First, between the decline of Greek culture and the rise of Islam, there had developed an important culture at once Greek but also a mixture of many Oriental elements—the Hellenistic civilization, which began to flower after 300 B.C. Its intellectual center was Alexandria, where a great institution of scientific research was established: the Museum. From it Hellenism radiated in every direction, becoming a vital influence on all who came into contact with it: the Egyptians, Syrians, Persians, and Arabs.

Greek philosophy had ended in A.D. 529 with Justianian's formal closing of the Academy of Athens. Many leading Neoplatonic philosophers took refuge at the Persian court of Kisra Anushirwan, and translated into Syriac and Persian the works they brought with them. This migration was a second channel through which Greek knowledge originating outside the homeland reached the Arab world and, later, Europe.

A third source was the Persian School of Jundishapur, the greatest center of intellectual exchange and syncretism in the sixth century A.D. It became a haven for the Nestorians expelled from Edessa in 489 as well as for the banished Neoplatonists. The Nestorians brought with them Syrian translations of many works, particularly medical ones. It was in Jundishapur that Kisra Anushirwan ordered the translation into Persian of some of the works of Artistotle and Plato. His own physician was sent to India in search of manuscripts and brought back not only many works on medical subjects but also the game of chess and the fables of Pilpay, or *Kalila wa Dimna*. Many fragments of Greek knowledge were translated or paraphrased at Jundishapur, which thus became a clearinghouse of philosophical and scientific ideas, its main purpose one of transmission rather than of creation.

A fourth factor was the activity of the Nestorians. In the first half of the fifth century A.D., the Syrian priest Nestorius was deposed and banished from Antioch to Arabia and later to Egypt. His disciples believed he had denied the complete mergence of the divine and human natures into one person in Christ, a distortion of his thought. His followers, devout and dedicated, emigrated east and into Edessa, where a school of medicine was flourishing. The school became the center of Nestorian influence and was succeeded by the School of Nisbis in Mesopotamia and, as related above, by the School of Jundishapur. Many Greek works on mathematics and medicine were translated into Syrian during the fifth century by the Christian Nestorians, who were, because of their polyglottism, especially fitted for this task. They all knew Greek and Syriac, and after the Moslem conquest, they were equally apt in Arabic. Some of them also knew Persian. They, more than any other people, helped to raise Islam to leadership in culture and science.

The last part of this century also witnessed the beginning of Syriac literature other than the translation of the Bible. This is a fifth significant factor, for that literature was one of the bridges over which Greek knowledge ultimately reached Europe. The earliest translation of Isagoge was composed about this time by the Nestorian Ibas.

Lastly, Sergios of Resaina, a sixth-century Syrian physician, philosopher, and translator from Greek into Syriac, introduced to his people many new treasures of Greek philosophy and medicine. His most important translations were of works by Plato, Aristotle, Porphyry, Hippocrates, and Galen (twenty-six books), and the Peripatetic treatise; he also translated some of the writings of Dionysios the Areopagite and possibly also the *Ars Grammatica* of Dionysios of Thrax. Some of his translations were revised in the ninth century by Hunain ibn Ishaq.

It was then that Moslem science came to the fore, filling the vacuum left by the decline of Western civilization, and from the late ninth century until the twelfth, Islamic influence on Western science and culture was very great.

The period A.D. 750-1400 produced some outstanding scholars of history. It was the most enlightened era of the pre-Renaissance world.

Our chronological survey begins with al Kindi. His work, like that of the others discussed in this book, reflects over one hundred fifty years of translation of Greek works into Arabic.

CHAPTER ONE

Early Scholars—Work and Influence

AL KINDI, "PHILOSOPHER OF THE ARABS"

Abu Yusuf Yakub ibn Ishaq al Kindi (died A.D. 873), known as "the philosopher of the Arabs," was the first Moslem philosopher and the only great philosopher of Arabian descent. An encyclopedic scientist, he was the author of many commentaries on mathematics, astrology, physics, medicine, pharmacy, geography, and music, only a few of which are extant, and of four books on the use of Hindu numbers. He translated many works from Greek into Arabic, and his study of Aristotle from the Neoplatonic point of view influenced Arab thinkers for generations. His two treatises on geometrical and physiological optics were utilized by Roger Bacon and the German physicist Witelo. Al Kindi was the first Moslem to write on music, his work containing a notation for the determination of pitch. He also wrote short treatises dealing mainly with ethics and political philosophy, such as *On Morals, On Facilitating the Paths to the Virtues, On the Warding Off of Griefs, On the Government of the Common People,* and *Account of the Intellect.*

Al Kindi's influence was so widely felt that Geronimo Cardano (1501-1576), the Italian physician and mathematician, considered him one of the twelve great minds of history.

AL FARGHANI

Al Farghani (died A.D. 870) has been called one of the greatest astronomers who ever lived. His most important work is *The*

11

Elements of Astronomy, which deals chiefly with celestial motion. This book, translated from Arabic into Latin as early as the twelfth century, was predominant in European astronomy. Al Farghani accepted the Ptolemaic theory and understood the value of the precession, believing that it is affected by the planets as well as the stars.

Paget Toynbee, nineteenth-century Oxford scholar and authority on Dante, showed Dante's indebtedness to al Farghani in the *Vita Nuova* and *Convivio.* After comparing selected passages and key captions in these works with selections from *The Elements of Astronomy,* Toynbee concluded that in the *Vita Nuova* Dante borrowed material dealing with the comparison of the planets, and that Dante's discussions of the distance of Venus from the earth, of poles and equators, of fixed stars, are based on al Farghani's writings. He adds: ". . . This treatise of al Farghani appears to have been a favorite with Dante and it is evident that he read it carefully, for he was largely indebted to it for astronomical and other data in *Convivio,* and elsewhere, though on only two occasions does he acknowledge his obligations."[1]

The Divine Comedy, too, follows al Farghani's astronomy, representing the eight revolving heavens approximately on the same scale of the logarithms of their dimensions estimated by al Farghani.

AL KHWARIZMI

Al Khwarizmi (died A.D. 850) is famous also among Western mathematicians. He also excelled in astronomy and geography and influenced mathematical thought.[2]

---

[1] Paget Toynbee, *Dante Studies and Research* (London, Methuen, 1902), pp. 56-77.

[2] George Sarton, *Introduction to the History of Science* (Baltimore, Williams and Wilkins, 1927-1948), Vol. I, p. 563.

AL RAZI

Al Razi is noted from his *The Spiritual Physic,* which shows him a thoughtful psychologist and outstanding physician. Some of his ideas have a strikingly modern ring:

Mutual helpfulness is closely related to division of labor. Each man must eat, be clothed, have shelter and security, though he may contribute directly to only one of these activities. The good life is thus attained by division of labor and mutual helpfulness. Each labors at a single task and is simultaneously servant and served, works for others and has others work for him. As a healthy and effective social organization is possible only on the basis of cooperation and mutual help, it is every man's duty to give assistance to his fellow man in one way or another and to work to the best of his abilities to that end, avoiding at the same time the two extremes of excess and deficiency.

If he toils all his life to earn more than he requires or needs for his old age without disposing of his earnings in such ways as will yield him comfort, he is really the loser and has enslaved himself; for he will have given away his own energy without obtaining in return a proper compensation. Such a man has not bartered toil against toil and service against service; his toil will have yielded profit only to his fellows, while their toil on his behalf will have passed him by.

The man who follows this rule in earning his living will have received in exchange toil for toil and service for service.[3]

Al Razi's expressions "cooperation," "mutual help," "mutual assistance" have had a revival in Pëtr Kropotkin's *Mutual Aid,* published in 1902 as refutation to Darwin's theory of the survival of the fittest. While the Darwinists declared competition and struggle for existence to be the governing law of nature, Kropotkin, like al Razi, emphasized the principle of mutual aid in which he no less saw a fundamental law of nature.

---

[3] Arthur J. Arberry, *The Spiritual Physick of Rhazes* (London, John Murray, 1950), pp. 89-90.

Al Razi also developed a pleasure-pain theory:

Pleasure consists in the restoration of that condition which preceded the suffering of pain. A man leaves a restful, shady spot to go out into the desert; there he proceeds under the hot summer sun, is affected by the heat; he goes back to his former place where he experiences pleasure until his body returns to its original condition. The intensity of his pleasure in coming home is in proportion to the intensity of the heat he had suffered.

Since pain sometimes sets in and increases gradually over a period of time, and the return to the original state often occurs quite suddenly, we do not become aware of the element of pain at once, while the sharpness of the return to the original state is keenly and pleasurably felt.

AL FARABI

Al Farabi (died A.D. 950) wrote widely in different fields. He wrote *Introduction to Logic* and *Abridgement of Logic;* his interest in natural science led to his commentaries on Aristotle's *Physics* and on the movement of the celestial bodies. He also wrote *The Power of the Soul, The Unity and the One, The Intelligence and the Intelligible,* and a commentary on Alexander's of Aphrodisias *De Animis.* He is also well known for his essays on substance, time, and space, and for various treatises, such as *The Gems of Wisdom, The Source of Questions,* and *The Knowledge of the Creator,* all of them dealing with problems of philosophy and theology. His work in the field of ethics includes a commentary on Aristotle's *Nicomachean Ethics.* In sociology he is known for *The Model City,* a work even now of sociological interest. His *Kitab al Musica* indicates that he had some considerable understanding of mensural notation and music theory in general. In this field al Farabi's work certainly equals, if it does not excel, any that has come down to us from the Greeks.[4]

---

[4] H. G. Farmer, in Sir Thomas Arnold and Alfred Guillaume, eds., *Legacy of Islam* (New York, Oxford University Press, 1931), pp. 356-376.

Al Farabi's philosophical system can be divided into three parts: logic; theoretical philosophy, in which metaphysics and psychology are discussed; and practical philosophy, dealing with problems of ethics and politics.[5]

In logic, al Farabi dealt with concepts, judgments, and reasoning. While he generally followed Aristotle, he also had original views of his own. Since the absence of black is a fact in the existence of white, we are tempted to say that every contrary is the absence of its contrary. Al Farabi states, however, that "if one deals with the science of something having a contrary that is more than a mere negation, then that science is not identical with that of its contrary. On the other hand, if we deal with the science of something having a contrary that is no more than its negation, then this science is one with that of its contrary, because in this case the two contraries are really and truly two relatives."

In theoretical philosophy he concerned himself wtih universal principles, which he defined as the ones found in many and affirmed of many. The inference is that the universal has no existence apart from the individual. The mind, in all its operations, he stated, exerts the functions of synthesizing the many in the one. We are not capable of understanding the meaning of a scene presented to our senses unless we unite its parts into a perceived whole. Perception involves synthesizing. Imagination involves analysis and synthesis, because nothing can be imagined without synthesizing the many in the one. The rendering of judgment, where one fact is affirmed of one thing or denied of

---

[5] Robert Hammond, *The Philosophy of al Farabi and Its Influence on Medieval Thought* (New York, Hobson Press, 1947). Extensive use has been made of this scholarly work in conjunction with al Farabi, *The Jami, (Collections)* which include *The Gems of Widsom; The Sources of Questions; A Letter in Reply to Questions; The Intellectual and the Intelligibles* (Cairo, Egypt, Saadeh Press, 1907); al Farabi, *Political Regime* (Cairo, Nile Press, 1927); and al Farabi, *Fusul al Madina,* ed. with English translation by D. M. Dunlop (New York, Cambridge University Press, 1961).

another, cannot take place except by synthesizing both terms, subjects and predicates, in one act of comparison. Further, the concept has a content, signifying the synthetic act of combining or organizing (by logical synthesis) parts or elements to form a whole—the universal, the one. The universal in reference to the particular is like genus and species in reference to individuals.

Al Farabi also discussed epistemological theology — knowability of God, proofs of God's existence, attributes of God; cosmology—relation of God to the world, eternity of matter, dualism of good and evil; the soul being distinct from the body, immortality of the human soul, we might say metaphysical psychology, which is of course not a medieval expression but is meant to denote the realm of supernatural concepts in terms of psychology.

In general psychology, al Farabi discussed powers of knowledge, sense knowledge, perceptive and abstractive knowledge, powers of action, sensitive and intellective appetite.

The last part of his work deals with ethics; actions, good, bad, or indifferent are considered along with his concept of a political society and an organization of the model state.

Of all his original works, al Farabi is best known for the *Encyclopedia,* a definition and brief account of all branches of science and art, and *The Political Regime,* also known as *The Book of Principles.*

The influence al Farabi exerted on medieval writers can be seen by a study of the work of Albertus Magnus, thirteenth-century theologian, philosopher, and teacher. St. Thomas Aquinas was among those who attended Albertus' lectures. In his writing, Albertus Magnus quoted quite freely from al Farabi, particularly on matters dealing with metaphysics. Albertus Magnus and St. Thomas Aquinas made it the goal of their lives to reconcile Aristotelian and Moslem philosophy with Christian theology. They discarded those of al Farabi's theories that conflicted with Christian teaching and adopted those that appeared to them reconcilable with Christianity. It should be remembered that the beginning of Scholasticism was contemporary with al Farabi. The following excerpts are taken from the Reverend Robert Hammond's pioneering work, *The Philosophy of Al Farabi and its Influence on Medieval Thought,* and from al Farabi's *Jami (The Collections)* and *The Political Regime.*

On proofs of God's existence, Hammond writes that "the arguments brought forth by al Farabi to prove that there is a God are three. These will be placed side by side with those of St. Thomas in order to aid the reader in comparing them. He will thus see the great similarity between them." [6]

PROOFS ADDUCED BY AL FARABI

PROOFS ADDUCED BY ST. THOMAS AQUINAS

1. *The Proof of Motion*

In this world there are things which are moved. Now, every object which is moved receives its motion from a mover. If the mover is itself moved, there must be another mover moving it, and after that still another and so on. But it is impossible to go on to infinity in the series of movers and things moved. Therefore, there must be an immovable mover, and this is God. (*The Jami*, pp. 70-71)

It is certain and evident to our senses that in the world some things are in motion. Now, whatever is in motion is put in motion by another. . . . If that by which it is put in motion be itself put in motion, then this also must needs be put in motion by another, and that by another again. But this cannot go on to infinity. . . . Therefore, it is necessary to arrive at a first mover, put in motion by no other; and this everyone understands to be God. (*Summa Theologica*, Part 1, Question 2, Article 3, p. 24)

---

[6] The following quotations from St. Thomas can be found in Thomas Aquinas, *Summa Theologica,* translated by Fathers of the English Dominican Province, 2d and rev. ed. (London, Burns, Oates and Washbourne, 1911), and in Thomas Aquinas, *Summa Contra Gentiles,* translated by the English Dominican Fathers from the latest Leonine edition (London, Burns, Oates and Washbourne, 1924). The extracts are identified in the text.

2. *Proof of Efficient Cause*

In contemplating the changeable world, one sees that it is composed of beings which have a cause, and this cause, in turn, is the cause of another. Now, in the series of efficient causes it is not possible to proceed to infinity. For, if A were the cause of B, B of C, C of D, and so on, here A would be the cause of itself, which is not admissible. Therefore, outside the series of efficient causes, there must be an uncaused efficient cause, and this is God. (*Ibid.*, pp. 115-125)

Another form of the same proof: Transition from not-being to being demands an actual cause. This cause either has its essence identical with its existence or not. If it does, then being is uncaused. If it does not, then existence must be from another, and that from another, and so on until we arrive at a First Cause, whose essence differs in no way from its existence. (*Ibid.*, p. 65)

In the world of sense we find there is an order of efficicient causes. There is no case known (neither is possible) in which a thing is found to be the efficient cause of itself. . . . Now, in efficient causes it is not possible to go on to infinity. . . . Therefore, it is necessary to admit a first efficient cause, to which everyone gives the name of God. (*Ibid.*, p. 25)

3. *Proof of Contingence*

[The third proof is based on the principle that all change must have a cause. To this effect al Farabi makes a distinction between a necessary being and a contingent being.] Contingent beings have had a beginning. Now, that which begins to exist must owe its existence to the action of a cause. This cause, in turn, ei-

We find in nature things that are possible to be and not to be. . . . But it is impossible for these always to exist. . . . Therefore, not all beings are merely possible, but there must exist something, the existence of which is necessary. But every necessary being either has its necessity caused by another or not, Now, it is impossible

ther is or is not contingent. If it is contingent, it also must have received its existence by the action of another cause, and so on. But a series of contingent beings which would produce one another cannot proceed to infinity or move in a circle. Therefore, the series of causes and effects must arrive at a cause that holds its existence from itself, and this is the first cause (ens primum). (*Ibid.*, p. 66)

to go on to infinity in necessary things which have their necessity caused by another. Therefore, we cannot but postulate the existence of some being having of itself its own necessity, and not receiving it from another, but rather causing in others their necessity. This all men speak of as God. (*Ibid.*, pp. 25-26)

Hammond adds that the different arguments provided by al Farabi to prove the existence of God are really one and the same, commonly called the cosmological argument, the validity of which is derived from the principle of causality. If the principle of causality is validly used to explain the phenomena of physics by the scientist, it must be regarded as validly employed by the philosopher to explain the universe. Thus the cosmological argument is valid because the principle of causality is valid. Aristotle's proof of an immovable mover, which leads to the conclusion that God is a designer and not a creator, was improved and corrected by al Farabi nearly three hundred years before the birth of St. Thomas Aquinas, who merely echoed the Moslem thinker.

Consideration of the attributes of God, too, shows al Farabi's influence on St. Thomas Aquinas.

ATTRIBUTES CONSIDERED BY
AL FARABI

ATTRIBUTES CONSIDERED BY
ST. THOMAS AQUINAS

Simplicity of God

God is simple because He is free from every kind of composition, physical or metaphysical. Physical composition may be either sub-

There is no composition in God. For, in every composite thing there must needs be act and potentiality . . . But in God there

stantial or accidental. It is substantial if the composite substance consists of body and soul, of matter and form. Now, an infinite being cannot be a substantial composite of matter and form, because this would mean that God results from the union of finite parts which would exist before Him in time, and therefore be the cause of His being. Nor can an accidental composition be attributed to the infinite, because this would imply a capacity for an increase in perfection, which the very notion of the infinite excludes. Therefore, there is not and cannot be any physical composition. (*Political Regime, op. cit.,* p. 39)

Neither can there be that kind of composition known as metaphysical, which results from the union of two different concepts so referred to the same real thing that neither one by itself signifies the whole reality as meant by their union. Thus, every contingent being is a metaphysical composite of essence and existence. Essence, as such, in reference to a contingent being implies its conceivableness or possibility, and abstracts from actual existence; while existence, as such, must be added to essence before we can speak of the being as actual. But the composite of essence and existence in a contingent being cannot be applied to the self-existent or infinite being in whom essence and existence are

is no potentiality. Therefore, in Him there is no composition . . . Every composite is subsequent to its components. Therefore, the first being, namely God, has no component parts. (*Summa Contra Gentiles,* First Book, Ch. XVIII, p. 39)

Existence denotes a kind of actuality . . . Now everything to which an act is becoming, and which is distinct from that act, is related thereto as potentiality to act . . . Accordingly if the divine essence is distinct from its existence, it follows that His essence and existence are mutually related as potentiality and act. Now it has been proved that in God there is nothing of potentiality, and that He is pure act. Therefore, God's essence is not distinct from His existence. (*Ibid.,* Ch. XXII, p. 55)

one. Therefore, there is no composition of essence and existence in God. (*The Jami,* pp. 115-125)

Nor can the composition of genus and difference, implied in the definition of man as a rational animal, be attributed to Him. For, God cannot be classified or defined, as contingent beings can. The reason is because there is not a single aspect in which He is perfectly similar to the finite, and consequently no genus in which He can be included. (*Ibid.,* p. 132)

Wherefore it is likewise evident that God cannot be defined: since every definition is composed of genus and difference. (*Ibid.,* Ch. XXV, p. 61)

Infinity of God

The uncaused being is infinite, For, if He were not, He would be limited, and therefore, caused, since the limit of a thing is the cause of it. But God is uncaused. Hence, it follows that the first being is infinite. (*Political Regime, op. cit.,* p. 7)

Being itself, considered absolutely infinite . . . Hence if we take a thing with finite being, this being must be limited by some other thing which is in some way the cause of that being. Now there can be no cause of God's being, since He is necessary of Himself. Therefore He has infinite being, and Himself is infinite. (*Ibid.,* Ch. XLIII, p. 96)

Immutability of God

God as the first cause is pure act, with the admixture of any potentiality, and for this reason He is not subject to any change. (*Ibid.,* p. 7)

It is shown that God is altogether immutable. First, because it was shown above that there is some first being, whom we call God; and that this first being must be pure act, without the admixture of any potentiality for the reason that, absolutely, potentiality is posterior to act. Now everything which is in any way changed, is in some way in potentiality. Hence it is evident that it is impossible for God to be in any way changeable. (*Summa Theologica,* Part 1, Question 9, Article 1, pp. 91-92)

Unity of God

God is only one. For, if there were two gods, they would have to be partly alike and partly different: in which case, however, the simplicity of each would be destroyed. In other words, if there were two gods, there would necessarily have to be some difference and some identity between them; the differential and the common element would constitute the parts of the essence of each one, and these parts, in turn, would be the cause of all; and then, not God, but His parts, would be the first being.

If there was anything equal to God, then He would cease to be the fullness of being, for fullness implies impossibility of finding anything of its kind. For instance, the fullness of power means inability of finding identical power anywhere else; the fullness of beauty means inability of finding identical beauty. Likewise if the first being possesses the fullness of being, this means that it is impossible to find anyone or anything identical with Him. Therefore, there is one infinite being, only one God.

If there be two things, both of which are of necessity, they must needs agree in the intention of the necessity of being. It follows, therefore, that they must be differentiated by something added either to one or to both of them; and consequently that either one is composite, or both. Now no composite exists necessarily per se. Therefore there cannot possibly be several things each of which exists necessarily; and consequently neither can there be several gods. (*Summa Contra Gentiles,* First Book, Ch. XLII, p. 90)

God comprehends in Himself the whole perfection of being. If then many gods existed, they would necessarily differ from each other. Something therefore would belong to one, which did not belong to another . . . So it is impossible for many gods to exist. (*Summa Theologica,* Part 1, Quesiton 11, Article 3, pp. 116-117)

God is existence itself. Consequently He must contain within Himself the whole perfection of being . . . It follows that the perfection of no one thing is wanting to God. (*Ibid.,* Question 4, Article 2, p. 48)

God is one, because He is free from all quantitative divisions. One means undivided. He who is indivisible in substance is one in essence. (*Ibid.*, pp. 3-8)

Since one is an undivided being, if anything is supremely one it must be supremely being, and supremely undivided. Now both of these belong to God. Hence it is manifest that God is one in the supreme degree. (*Ibid.*, Question 11, Article 4, p. 118)

Intelligence of God

God is intelligent. A thing is intelligent because it exists without matter. Now, God is absolutely immaterial. Therefore, He is intelligent. (*Ibid.*, p. 8)

A thing is intelligent from the fact of its being without matter. Now it was shown above that God is absolutely immaterial. Therefore He is intelligent. (*Summa Contra Gentiles*, First Book, Ch. XLIV p. 100)

God knows Himself perfectly. If there is anything that would keep God from knowing Himself, that would be matter. But God is absolutely immaterial. Hence it follows that He knows Himself fully, because His intellect is His essence.

That which by its nature is severed from matter and from material conditions, is by its very nature intelligible. Now every intelligible is understood according as it is actually one with the intelligent; and God is Himself intelligent, as we have proved. Therefore since He is altogether immaterial, and is absolutely one with Himself, He understands Himself most perfectly.

That which by its essence is intellect in act, is too, by its very essence intelligible in act. Now, the divine intellect is always intellect in act, because if it were not so, then it would be in potentiality with respect to its object; and this is impossible. Just exactly the opposite occurs in man. The human intellect is not always in act. Man knows himself in act after knowing himself potentially.

A thing is actually understood through the unification of the intellect in act and the intelligible in act. Now the divine intellect is always intellect in act. . . . Since the divine intellect and the divine essence are one, it is evident that God understands Himself perfectly: for God is both His own intellect and His own essence. (*Ibid.*, Ch. XLVII, p. 105)

The reason for this is that man's intellect is not his essence. Hence, what he knows does not belong to him by essence. (*Ibid.*, pp. 8-9)

God Knows All Things through Knowledge of Himself

It must not be said that God derives His knowledge of things from the things themselves, but rather it must be said that He knows things through His essence. By looking at His essence, He sees everything. Hence, knowing His essence is the cause of His knowing other things. (*The Jami, op. cit.*, p. 170)

So we say that God sees Himself in Himself, because He sees Himself through His essence; and He sees other things, not in themselves, but in Himself; inasmuch as His essence contains the similitude of things other than Himself. (*Summa Theologica*, Part 1, Question 14, Article 5, p. 190)

God Is Truth

Truth follows being, namely, truth and being coincide. But God is the supreme being. Therefore, He is the supreme truth. Truth is the conformity of the intellect and thing. But in God intellect and object of thought are one and the same. (*The Political Regime, op. cit.*, pp. 10-11)

Truth and being are mutually consequent upon one another; since the Truth is when that is said to be which is, and that not to be, which is not. Now God's being is first and most perfect. Therefore His truth is also first and supreme—Truth is in our intellect through the latter being equated to the thing understood. Now the cause of equality is unity. Since then in the divine intellect, intellect and thing understood are absolutely the same. His truth must be the first and supreme truth. (*Summa Contra Gentiles*, First Book, Ch. LXII, pp. 131-132)

God Is Life

Just as we call ourselves living beings, because we have a nature capable of sensation or understanding, in like manner God, whose intellect is His essence, must have life in the most perfect degree. (*Ibid.*, p. 11)

Wherefore that being whose act of understanding is its very nature, must have life in the most perfect degree. (*Summa Theologica*, Part 1, Question 18, Article 3, p. 255)

Hammond adds that al Farabi's carefully worked-out treatise on the question of God's existence and His attributes agrees so perfectly with the Christian viewpoint that the whole topic might have been written by a Christian Father, rather than by a Moslem. Hammond therefore concludes that "it is evident that al Farabi's theology exerted a great influence on medieval thinkers, because upon comparing the teachings of al Farabi with those of St. Thomas, we see without doubt the influence of the former on the latter but not vice versa." [7]

Here is further evidence of al Farabi's influence on St. Thomas Aquinas.

AL FARABI

ST. THOMAS AQUINAS

Theory of Knowledge

Every idea comes from sense-experience according to the adage "There is nothing in the intellect that has not first been in the senses." The mind is like a smooth tablet on which nothing is written.

Now, sense is a passive power, and is naturally changed by the exterior sensible. Wherefore the exterior cause of such change is what is directly perceived by the sense, and according to the di-

---

[7] Hammond, *op. cit.*, p. 29.

It is the senses that do all the writing on it. The senses are five: sight, hearing, smell, taste, and touch. Each of these has a proper sensible thing for its object. In every sensation the sense receives the form or species of sensible things without the matter, just as wax receives the form of a seal without any of the matter of it. (*The Jami, op. cit.*, p. 149)

versity of that exterior cause are the sensitive powers diversified.

Now, change is of two kinds, one natural and the other spiritual. Natural change takes place by the form of the changer being received, according to its natural existence, into the thing changed, as heat is received into the thing heated. Whereas spiritual change takes place by the form of the changer being received, according to a spiritual mode of existence, into the thing changed, as the form of color is received into the pupil which does not thereby become colored. Now, for the operation of the senses, a spiritual change is required, whereby an intention of the sensible form is effected in the sensible organ. (*Ibid.*, Part 1, Third Number [Questions LXXV-CXIX] and Question LXXVIII, Article 3, p. 80)

Theory of Sense Knowledge

The sensations we have once experienced are not utterly dead. They can reappear in the form of images. The power by which we revive a past sensible experience without the aid of any physical stimulus is called imagination (*el-motakhayilah*).

The power by which we combine and divide images is called the cogitative (*el-mofakarah*). If we were limited merely to the experience of our actual sensations, we would have only the present, and

For the retention and preservation of these forms (sensible forms), the phantasy or imagination is appointed which are the same, for phantasy or imagination is as it were a storehouse of forms received through the senses. Furthermore, for the apprehension of intentions which are not received through the senses, the estimative power is appointed: and for the preservation thereof, the memorative power, which is a storehouse of such like intentions.

with it there would be no intellectual life at all. But fortunately we
are endowed with the power of
calling back a former experience,
and this is called memory (*el-
hafizah—el-zakirah*).[8] (*The Jami,
op. cit.*, pp. 150-176)

(*Ibid.*, Question LXXVIII, Article 4, p. 85)

Among the internal senses al Farabi also mentions instinct, or
el-uahm (the estimative power of the Scholastics), by which
animals seek what is useful to them and avoid what is harmful.
"It is by this faculty," he says, "that the sheep knows that the
wolf is an enemy and that the little lambs need care and
attention."

On consideration of the intellect proper (the speculative intellect, an apprehensive power relating to what is above itself,
and the practical intellect, a motive power referring to what is
below itself, namely, the world of the senses that it must govern),
al Farabi treats the speculative intellect as consisting of the
four faculties of the soul: the passive intellect, the active intellect, the acquired intellect, and the actual intellect. Hammond
then offers the following parallels:

AL FARABI

The passive intellect or *aql
hayulani* is in potentiality to
things intelligible. It passes from
potentiality to act when it sep-
arates mentally the essence from
its individuating notes. This essence, abstracted from the individuals, becomes actually the
intelligible form or species which
is one and the same as the intellect in act.

ST. THOMAS AQUINAS

The human intellect is in potentiality with regard to things intelligible, and is at first like a clean
tablet on which nothing is written.
This is made clear from the fact
that at first we are only in potentiality to understand and after-
wards we are made to understand
actually. And so it is evident that
with us to understand is in a way
to be passive, and consequently

---

[8] *Ibid.*, pp. 38-39; Al Farabi, *The Jami, op. cit.*, pp. 150-175.

When forms existing in matter outside the soul become actually intelligible, their existence as actually intelligible is not the same as forms existing in matter. For forms existing in matter (individualized concretely) are associated with the various categories of time and place, quantity and quality, but they are stripped of these individuating conditions the moment they become actually intelligible. (*Ibid., op. cit.,* pp. 49-54)

The active intellect, or *aql faal* of which Aristotle speaks in the *Anima III,* is immaterial. . . . it causes the passive intellect to pass from potentiality to act, and makes the intelligible in potentiality intelligible in act.

The active intellect is related to the passive as the sun is to the eye. The eye is in potentiality to see while it is dark, but it sees actually only as soon as light shines. The same is to be said of both the passive and active intellect.

The active intellect shines a kind of light upon the passive, by which the passive becomes actual, (*aql bilfil*) and the intelligible in potentiality becomes intelligible

the intellect is a passive power. (*Ibid.,* Question LXXIX, Article 2, p. 92)

Nothing is reduced from potentiality to act except by something in act; as the senses are made actual by what is actually sensible. We must therefore assign on the part of the intellect, some power, to make things actually intelligible, by the abstraction of the species from material conditions. And such is the necessity for an active intellect. (*Ibid.,* Article 3, p. 94)

The intellectual soul is indeed actually immaterial, but it is in potentiality to determinate species. On the contrary, phantasms are actual images of certain species, but are immaterial in potentiality. Wherefore nothing prevents one and the same soul, inasmuch as it is actually immaterial, having one power by which it makes things actually immaterial, by abstraction from the conditions of individual matter: which power is called the active intellect; and another power, receptive of such species, which is called the passive intellect by reason of its being in potentiality to such species. (*Ibid.,* Article 4, p. 98)

Not only does the active intellect throw light on the phantasm; it does more. By its own power it abstracts the intelligible species from the phantasm. It throws light

in act. Furthermore, the active intellect is a separate substance, which, by lighting up the phantasms, makes them to be actually intelligible.

The acquired intellect or *aql mustafad* is simply the actual intellect developed under the inspiration of the active intellect. Albertus Magnus calls it "Intellect adeptus." (*Ibid., op. cit.*, pp. 54-56)

[Al Farabi's theory may be summed up as follows: the intellect, in its primitive state, is a power of the soul. Since it has only a potential existence, he calls it *aql hayulani*, the material intellect. For, like matter, it has the capacity for taking on a new form. In fact, the material or passive intellect passes from potentiality to actuality when it abstracts the essence from the individuals. But what is the force that causes the passive intellect to pass from potentiality to act? It is, according to al Farabi, the active intellect, a separate substance, emanating from God, which is able to awaken the latent power in man and arouse it to activity.]

on the phantasm, because, just as the sensitive part acquires a greater power by its conjunction with the intellectual part, so by the power of the active intellect the phantasms are made more fit for the abstraction therefrom of intelligible intentions. Furthermore, the active intellect abstracts the intelligible species from the phantasm, forasmuch as by the power of the active intellect we are able to disregard the conditions of individuality, and to take into our consideration the specific nature, the image of which informs the passive intellect. (*Ibid.*, Question LXXXV, Article 1, p. 183)

[St. Thomas Aquinas' theory boils down to this: to abstract the essence and to perceive it are two acts specifically distinct; therefore they demand two distinct powers. Hence the soul requires one power which renders the essences of sensible things actually intelligible by stripping them of their material conditions in which they exist, which power is called the active intellect, and another power by which it comprehends the intelligible; this is called the passive intellect because of its being in potentiality to all intelligibles.][9]

---

[9] *Ibid.*, pp. 42-44; and al Farabi, The *Jami, op. cit.*, pp. 49-56.

Thus, as Hammond concludes, St. Thomas Aquinas depended on al Farabi for his arguments to prove the existence of God and to show how His nature can be perceived. He also borrowed from the earlier thinker his theories of essence and existence and of being. Further, St. Thomas' teacher, Albertus Magnus, quoted the Farabian definition of the universal, proving beyond doubt that the Christian scholars were familiar with the writings of our philosopher.[10]

Surely Hammond proved his point:

> My efforts will have been amply rewarded if this book enables the reader to find through its pages two facts: first, that al Farabi was well acquainted with Greek philosophy; so well acquainted in fact, that he was able, through diligent study, to perfect some its old theories and work out new ones; second, that the schoolmen (Albertus Magnus and St. Thomas and others) borrowed from him a great amount of material which hitherto has been regarded by many as a product of their speculation, while in reality it is not. In justice to al Farabi, and other Arabian thinkers, we should candidly admit that Christian philosophy owes a great deal to them.[11]

Al Farabi also wrote on practical philosophy. In his *Political Regime* he expressed ideas on political society and the model state.

AL KHWARIZMI

Muhammad ibn Ahmad al Khwarizmi (fl. A.D. 950-976) wrote *The Keys of Science*, a book important for the study of Moslem culture of his time. He divided the sciences into two groups, the first comprising theology, poetry, history, jurisprudence, administration, grammar, and secretarial art, and the second including logic, geometry, arithmetic, mechanics, medicine, and music. There is no English translation of *The Keys of Science*.

---

[10] *Ibid.*, p. 11.
[11] *Ibid.*, Preface.

CHAPTER TWO

Eleventh-Century Learning

AL BIRUNI

Al Biruni (died 1048) was a philosopher, mathematician, astronomer, geographer, and encyclopedist, one of the great scientists of Islam. In his *Chronology of Ancient Nations*, or *Vestige of the Past*, written about A.D. 1000, he treated of the calendars and the eras of ancient peoples. Among his main works are *History of India* and *An Astronomical Encyclopedia and a Summary of Mathematics, Astronomy, and Astrology*. In these works al Biruni, five hundred years before Galileo, considered the question whether or not the earth rotates around its axis; he did not, however, reach a definite conclusion. His scientific contributions include an explanation of the working of natural springs and artesian wells by the hydrostatic principles of communicating vessels, and an estimate of the speed of light in which he calculated it must be immensely greater than the speed of sound. He also worked in the field of specific gravity. Following is a description of the method he used in conducting an experiment:

> First he weighed a body in air, then he weighed the same body in water, by placing it in a conical vessel with a hole drilled in it at a certain height. Thereafter he weighed the water which the body had displaced, and from the weight of the water displaced he knew the mass of the body. Then by dividing the weight of the body in air by the weight of the displaced water he arrived at the specific gravity of the body, or, to be more precise, of the substance of which the body was formed.[1]

IBN AL HAITHAM

Ibn al Haitham (died 1039) was a leading physicist and a trailblazer in optics. His work showed substantial progress in

---

[1] Omar A. Farrukh, *The Arab Genius in Science and Philosophy*, tranlated by John B. Hardie (Washington, D.C., American Council of Learned Societies, 1945), p. 62.

the use of the experimental method. His main work, *Kitab al Manazir (Optics)*, was the first scientific description of the eye; he also attempted to explain binocular vision. He tried to measure the height of the atmospheric layer above the surface of the earth, basing his calculations on the belief that twilight begins to fade when the sun stands 19 degrees below the horizon. His studies on the refraction and reflection of light enabled him to explain the apparently larger size of the sun and moon at their rising and setting, and he stated the principle of the spherical path of light rays.

Farrukh [2] has traced al Haitham's considerable influence on a number of later Western scholars, an influence strengthened by the fact that his works were translated before the advent of the Renaissance. Al Haitham is still known as the author of *"Questions on the Eye"*. John Peckham's late-thirteenth century book on optics is no more than an excerpt from Ibn al Haitham's work, while exact echoes of *Kitab al Manazir* are found in Witelo's *Optics*, utilized by Johannes Kepler. Roger Bacon, founder of experimental science, probably made use of the Arabic original of al Haitham's work as well as of its Latin translations.

AL MAWARDI

Al Mawardi, who lived in Basra and Baghdad in the eleventh century, was a student of politics. His main works were *Kitab al Ahkam al Sultaniya (Book on the Principles of Government)* and a treatise on ethics, *Kitab Adab al Dunya Wal Din*, still popular in Turkish and Egyptian schools. In acknowledging his indebtedness to Moslem writers on the subject of government and politics, ibn Khaldun (Chapter 5) referred to al Mawardi's works and especially to *Principles of Government*, which is a compilation of basic principles of political law and administration, and government policy on setting the value of money and tariffs. Al Mawardi's work is not available in English.

---

[2] *Ibid.*, p. 67.

IBN SINA

Ibn Sina (died 1036), known in Europe as Avicenna, was the most famous social and natural scientist of Islam. He also represents the climax of medieval philosophy. Like Aristotle and Vergil, he was considered a magician by people of subsequent generations. His eminence was such that it almost discouraged other scholars' investigations. In him Arab science reached its climax.[3] Yet, very little of ibn Sina's work has been translated into English.

Ibn Sina has been credited with ninety-nine books dealing with philosophy, medicine, geometry, astronomy, theology, philology, and art. He is most celebrated for his *Kitab al Shifa (Book of Healing)*, in which he divided practical knowledge into ethics, economics, and politics, and theoretical knowledge into physics, mathematics, and metaphysics.

His most important contribution was probably his *Qanun Fil-Tibb (Canon of Medicine)*, a medical encyclopedia of about one million words, which remained supreme in the West for over six centuries and was used as a textbook down to the advent of modern medicine.

There is some evidence that Leonardo da Vinci used ibn Sina's work or intended to use it, for at least four references to ibn Sina are made in Leonardo's notebooks. In one, Leonardo wrote, "Have a translation made of Avicenna: on the utilities—the book on the science of machines precedes the book on the Utilities." [4] Dante placed ibn Sina in the illustrious company of Hippocrates, Galen, and Scaliger, the great sixteenth-century Italian physician; he considered him superior to Galen in philosophy.

---

[3] Philip K. Hitti, *History of the Arabs,* 6th ed. (New York, Macmillan, 1955), p. 367.

[4] Leonardo Da Vinci, *The Notebook*, translated by Edward MacCurdy (New York, George Braziller, 1955), p. 1173; other references to ibn Sina appear on pp. 107, 172, 1170.

His writings, as well as those of other philosophers and scientists of medieval Islam, not only formed a bridge between ancient Greece and Renaissance Europe, but also constituted a distinctive school of epistemology and metaphysics.

Ibn Sina believed in one God, the doctrine of prophetic inspiration, and the authority of Mohammed. In the battle between free thought and orthodox belief al Ghazzali with his *Tahafut al Falasifa (Incoherence of Philosophers)* ended the possibility of ibn Sina's system providing the pattern for a broader Islamic theology.

Ibn Sina's influence was deep and lasting. It reached out to Spain to make its mark on two great minds—ibn Rushd and Maimonides—and into Latin Christendom to the Scholastics. It is remarkable to what extent the thinking of Albertus Magnus and Thomas Aquinas was influenced by ibn Sina. Roger Bacon called him "the chief authority in philosophy after Aristotle," and Aquinas spoke with as much respect of him as of Plato.

CHAPTER THREE

Islamic Learning in the Twelfth Century

AL GHAZZALI

Al Ghazzali (1058-1111), theologian and apologist of Islam, was one of its most original thinkers. He exerted great influence upon Jewish and Christian scholasticism and succeeded in reconciling his pragmatic tendencies with strict Moslem orthodoxy.[1] He studied under al Juwayni, the greatest theologian of his age. Nizam al Mulk, all-powerful vizier of the Turkish Sultan, who ruled the Abbasid caliphate of Baghdad, appointed al Ghazzali professor of philosophy in the Nizamiyah College at Baghdad. At the age of thirty-three, al Ghazzali had attained one of the most distinguished positions in the academic world of his day.

Four years later, al Ghazzali met a religious crisis. He had come to feel that the one thing that mattered was the avoidance of Hell and the attainment of Paradise. His own way of life he saw as too worldly, and he left Baghdad to take up the life of a wandering ascetic. He returned a year later to resume teaching, but he was completely changed. Now, at thirty-eight, he was deeply religious and could hope that his pious life would earn him eternal reward. He died at the age of fifty-three.

---

[1] George Sarton, *Introduction to the History of Science* (Baltimore, Williams and Wilkins, 1927-1948), Vol. I., p. 753. Some of al Ghazzali's work has been translated into English by W. Montgomery Watt; Claud Field, H. A. Homes; W. H. T. Gardner; D. B. MacDonald; W. R. Gardner, and others.

W. Montgomery Watt's penetrating study of al Ghazzali's work, particularly *Deliverance from Error,* led him to conclude that al Ghazzali introduces his discussion in a manner reminiscent of Descartes. The bond of mere authority ceased to hold him, as they ceased to hold the father of modern European philosophy. Looking for necessary truths, al Ghazzali, like Descartes, came to doubt the infallibility of sense perception and to rest his philosophy rather on principles which are intuitively certain.[2] Al Ghazzali divided seekers of truth into four distinct groups:

1. *Theologians,* who succeeded in attaining the aims of theology but who did not go far enough in the elucidation of their doctrines. These he regarded as inadequate.

2. *Philosophers,* of three classes: materialists, irreligious because they deny the Creator; naturalists, believing in God but irreligious because they did not believe in the Last Day; and freethinkers, the worst and by far the most dangerous. They included Socrates, Plato, and Aristotle as well as al Farabi and ibn Sina, contemporary rivals whose philosophies were a form of Neoplatonism adapted to Islamic monotheism. The work of these men he rejected completely.

3. *Authoritarians,* who held that truth is to be attained not by reason but by accepting the pronouncement of the infallible Imam. Al Ghazzali showed the falsity of their views, scorning them for following others blindly. He encouraged independent judgment in religious affairs as well as in all other matters.[3]

4. *Mystics.* Al Ghazzali accepted mysticism and practiced it after his brief stay at the University of Baghdad. He set forth his own mystical experience.

> When I had done with these sciences [all except mysticism], I turned with set purpose to mysticism. I knew that the complete mystic way includes both belief and practical activity; it includes

---

[2] W. Montgomery Watt, *The Faith and Practice of Al Ghazzali* (London, Allen and Unwin, 1953), p. 12.

[3] *Ibid.,* p. 48.

getting rid of the obstacles in the self and in stripping off its base characteristics and vicious morals, so that the heart may attain to freedom from what is not God and to constant recollection of Him.

Intellectual belief was easier to me than practical activity. I began to acquaint myself with beliefs of the mystics by reading their books. . . . I thus comprehended their fundamental teaching and progressed . . . in the knowledge of mysticism. It became clear to me, however, that what is most distinctive of mysticism is something which cannot be apprehended by study, but only by immediate experience [literally, *tasting*], by ecstasy, and by a moral change. What a difference there is between *knowing* the definition of health and satiety, together with their causes and presuppositions, and being healthy and satisfied! What a difference between being acquainted with the definition of drunkenness—namely, that it designates a state arising from the domination of the seat of the intellect by vapors arising from the stomach—and being drunk! Indeed, the drunken man while in that condition does not know the definition of drunkenness nor the scientific account of it. The sober man, on the other hand, knows the definition of drunkenness and its basis, yet he is not drunk in the very least. Again, the doctor, when he is himself ill, knows the definition and causes of health and the remedies which restore it and yet is lacking in health. Similarly, there is a difference between knowing the true nature and causes and conditions of the ascetic life and actually leading such a life and forsaking the world.

It became clear to me that the mystics were men who had had real religious experiences, not men just of words, and that I had already progressed as far as is possible by way of intellectual apprehension. What remained for me could not be attained by oral instruction and study but only by immediate experience and by walking in the mystic way. . . . Now from the sciences [theology and philosophy] . . . there had to come to me a sure faith (a) in God most high, (b) in prophethood as revelation, and (c) in the Last Day. These three credal principles were firmly rooted in my being, not through any carefully argued proofs, but by reason of various causes, coincidences and experiences which are not capable of being stated in words.

It had already become clear to me that I had no hope for the bliss of the world to come, save through a God-fearing life and the withdrawal of myself from vain desires. It was clear to me, too, that the way to all this was to sever the attachment of the heart to worldly things by leaving the mansion of deception and returning to that of eternity and to advance toward God most high with all earnestness. It was clear that this was only to be achieved by turning away from wealth and position and fleeing from all time-consuming entanglement.

Next, I considered the circumstances of my life, and realized that I was caught in a veritable thicket of attachment. I also considered my activities, of which the best were my teaching and lecturing, and realized that even in them I was dealing with sciences that were unimportant and contributed nothing to the attainment of eternal life.

After that I examined my motive in my work of teaching and realized that it was not a pure desire for the things of God, but that the impulse moving me was the desire for an influential position and public recognition. I saw for certain that I was on the brink of a crumbling bank of sand and in imminent danger of hell-fire unless I set about to mend my ways.

I reflected on this continuously for a time. . . . One day I would form a resolution to quit Baghdad and get rid of these circumstances; the next day I would abandon my resolution. I put one foot forward and drew the other back. If in the morning I had a genuine longing to seek eternal life, by the evening the attack of a whole host of desires had reduced it to impotence. Worldly desires were striving to keep me by their chains just where I was, while the voice of faith was calling, "To the road! To the road! . . . all that keeps you busy, both intellectually and practically, is but hypocrisy and delusion" . . . but Satan would return [saying] "This is a passing mood . . . do not yield . . . for if you leave [your] this influential position, these comfortable and dignified circumstances . . . this state of safety and security . . . you will not find it easy to return to all this."

For nearly six months I was continuously tossed about between the attraction of world desires and the impulse toward eternal life. In that month the matter ceased to be one of choice and became one of compulsion. God caused my tongue to dry up so that I was prevented from lecturing. One particular day I would make an effort to lecture in order to gratify the hearts of my following, but my tongue would not utter a single word nor could I accomplish anything at all.

This impediment in my speech produced grief in my heart, and at the same time the power to digest and assimilate food and drink was impaired: I could hardly swallow or digest a single mouthful of food. My powers became so weakened that the doctors gave up all hope of successful treatment. "This trouble arises from the heart," they said, "and from there it has spread through the constitution; the only method of treatment is to allay the anxiety which has come over the heart."

Thereupon, perceiving my impotence, and having altogether lost my power of choice, I sought refuge with God most high as one who is driven to Him. He answered me . . . and made it easy for my heart to turn away from position and wealth; from children and friends. . . .

In general, then, how is a mystic way described? . . . The first condition is the purification of the heart completely from what is other than God most high; the key to it . . . is the sinking of the heart completely in the recollection of God and the end of it is complete absorption in God. . . .

With this first stage of the "way," there begin the revelations and visions. The mystics in their working state now behold angels and the spirits of the prophets; they hear these speaking and are instructed by them. Later a higher state is reached; instead of beholding forms and figures, they come to stages in the "way" which it is hard to describe in language; if a man attempts to express these, his words inevitably contain what is clearly erroneous.

In general what they manage to achieve is nearness to God; some, however, would conceive of this as "inherence" [*hulul*], some as "union" [*ittihad*], and some as "connection" [*Wusul*]. All this is erroneous. In my book, *The Noblest Aim,* I have explained the nature of the error here. Yet he who has attained the mystic "state" need do no more.

Al Ghazzali's books, especially *Revival of the Religious Sciences,* were translated into Latin before 1150—about forty years after his death. His influence on theology therefore was relatively immediate and George F. Moore stated that the personal influence of al Ghazzali on the science of theology was greater than that of St. Thomas Aquinas.[4] Since al Ghazzali placed

---

[4] George F. Moore, *History of Religion* (New York, Scribner's, 1919), Vol. II, p. 457.

science, philosophy, and reason in positions inferior to religion and theology, the Scholastics accepted his views, which became characteristic of most medieval philosophy. Further, al Ghazzali held that events are brought about by the will of God rather than by external causes. He therefore denied the principle of causality. This view was adopted by the English thinker David Hume (1711-1776), who defined the relationship of cause and effect as the result of recollections rather than of principle, emphasizing that even though one event follows another, the first is not a priori the cause of the second. While al Ghazzali referred the ultimate ground to God, Hume referred the ultimate ground to recollections. The similarity of al Ghazzali's and Hume's thinking on this subject prompted Ernest Renan, the eminent French historian, to remind his readers, "Hume has said [about the causal nexus] nothing more than al Ghazzali had already said." [5]

After becoming a mystic, al Ghazzali laid down for himself rules of conduct and set them forth in *The Ten Rules,* a summary of his ethics.

Intention, he declared, is the first rule of conduct. This intention should be good and stable, good insofar as it tries at all times to accomplish its objective, leaving the rest to God, and stable insofar as it continues to be good, that is, persists in seeking its objective without being dissuaded from it by anything *worldly.*

Al Ghazzali's second rule is unity of purpose. This involves preparing for the *hereafter,* to be done only by *serving God alone.* We know we are serving God when we are satisfied only with the truth and when we deem everything else unworthy.

---

[5] Omar A. Farrukh, *The Arab Genius in Science and Philosophy,* translated by John B. Hardie (Washington, D. C., American Council of Learned Societies, 1945), pp. 93-94.

Realizing that this is a difficult rule to follow in a *world where man is tempted at all times* to become the slave of false values, and having himself earlier doubted the goodness of this rule, al Ghazzali warns against doubt as the most painful and deadly of all diseases. The outward sign of obedience to this rule is to prefer the hereafter to worldly affairs.

His third rule is conformity to *truth,* even at the expense of forsaking pleasure, by resisting desire and *renouncing luxury* and ease.

In his fourth rule al Ghazzali urged *orthodoxy* among Moslems. He believed that the variety of doctrines and sects divided men, fostered hatred, and led to the saving of no one. He therefore insisted that Moslems conform to established practice and *avoid all innovations* in religion.

The fifth rule forbids procrastination and urges daily examination of one's duties and actions.

In his sixth rule al Ghazzali reminded his fellow men that they were incapable of doing anything without the help of God, that they should acknowledge that fact daily but not use it as a pretext for laziness in good works or neglect of independent action.

Al Ghazzali's seventh rule is one of fear and hope in which he preached salvation by faith.

The eighth rule recommends a life of devotion and prayer. To neglect devotional exercises is to shut oneself from the only source of spiritual power.

The ninth rule calls for continual observation and watchfulness. He who persists in meditating about God and banishes from his heart everything but Him will find God and will move from groping to tranquillity, from tranquillity to reality, and finally will attain true faith.

Al Ghazzali's tenth rule is consecration to a knowledge wherein one may see God. This rule should be pursued with diligence, both outwardly and inwardly. Its outward sign is perseverance in good works, since he who thinks that he can do without good works is a moral bankrupt.[6]

Al Ghazzali's *Ihya Ulum al Dinn (Revival of Religious Science)*, mentioned earlier, is divided into four major parts. The first deals with the act of worship, the second with the usage of life, the third with the destructive matters of life, and the fourth with the saving matters of life. In the *Ihya*, al Ghazzali preserved the summation of Moslem thought.

Al Ghazzali's other leading works are *Kitab Tahafut al Falasifa (Destruction,* or *Vanity,* or *Incoherence of Philosophers)*, referred to earlier in connection with ibn Sina; *Mishkat al Anwar (The Niche of Light);* and *Al Munquidh Minal Dalal (The Deliverance from Error)*, from which we have already quoted.

Raymond Martin, a thirteenth-century Catalan Dominican scholar, understood Arabic and had access to *The Incoherence of Philosophers,* a polemic against the philosophers and scholastics of Islam; he incorporated a great deal of it into his *Pugio Fidei (The Sword of Faith).* Thereafter al Ghazzali's arguments in favor of the *creato ex nihilo* and that God's knowledge comprises particulars, as well as his arguments in support of the dogma of the resurrection of the dead were employed by Christians in many Scholastic treatises.

> Another work of al Ghazzali, which treats of the place of reason as applied to revelation, presents many parallels in its arguments and conclusions with the *Summa Theologica* of St. Thomas Aquinas. This can hardly have more than one explanation, since the *Summa* and the *Pugio Fidei* (The Sword of Faith) were both written at the request of the Dominican Order. The similarity of some chapters in both is suggestive. Some of the more important questions on which Aquinas and Al Ghazzali agree are the value of human reason in explaining or demonstrating the truth about divine things; the ideas of contingency and necessity as demonstrating the existence of God; the unity of God

---

[6] Nabih Faris, in Philip K. Hitti and others, *The Arab Heritage* (Princeton, N. J., Princeton University Press, 1944), pp. 142-158.

as implied in His perfection; the possibility of beatific vision; divine knowledge and divine simplicity; the names of God; miracle as a testimony to the truth of utterances of prophets; and the dogma of the resurrection of the dead.[7]

Another source for Aquinas' familiarity with the writings of al Ghazzali was Maimonides, who drew some of his theories from the *Maqasid al Falasifah (Aims of Philosophers)* of al Ghazzali: Aquinas refers in *Summa Contra Gentiles,* iii, 97, to a Moslem theologian quoted by Maimonides. That theologian is al Ghazzali.

Bar Hebraeus, the brilliant thirteenth-century Jacobite whose rebellious attitude paralled that of al Ghazzali, reflects the influence of al Ghazzali in his *Book of the Dove* and his *Ethikon.*

As a result of his ethical teachings, al Ghazzali's influence on medieval Judaism was even greater than his influence on Christian Scholasticism. He approached Jewish ethical ideals so closely that he was seen by many actually to be drifting toward Judaism. His works were eagerly studied by Jewish writers, some borrowing extensively from them. His *Mizan al Amal (Value of Meditation)* was translated into Hebrew and clothed in Jewish garb by the substitution of Biblical and Talmudic quotations for Quranic and Hadith ones.[8]

Al Ghazzali's ethical code served the old and the young as guide. In a minor but original and most delightful book, *Ayyuha-L-Walad (Guide to the Young),* he offered advice through an old scholar.

A very learned and cultured scholar reminded himself that he had spent his entire life learning, teaching, and collecting books and that now the time had come for him to separate that knowledge of his that would benefit him after death from that knowledge which would not. The former he planned to keep, the

---

[7] *Ibid., p.* 156.
[8] *Ibid.,* pp. 155-157.

latter to forget. He then sought al Ghazzali's advice, planning
to write it down.

Al Ghazzali offered many precepts through this elderly scholar.
The theme running through the guide is that material things
are not lasting; they should not be sought, and a minimum of
them should suffice. Man's main work should be to prepare himself for the hereafter.

> Young man, don't be without a job; don't be without some-
> thing important to do. And remember that you can't *do* without
> *learning*, and you can't *learn* without *doing*. And remember, too,
> that *learning* is one thing and *doing* is another. That is, if one
> does not practice what he learns, his learning is useless. The
> following will illustrate what I mean: A brave warrior is in
> the desert and has ten swords and other arms. He is suddenly
> attacked by a ferocious lion. Now what do you think happens!
> Will his swords and his other arms protect him from the lion if
> he does not know how to use them? Similarly if a man has read
> thousands of things and learned them and did not do any of them
> they would not do him any good. Also, if you have read and
> have learned that which you have read for a hundred years,
> and if you collected thousands of books, you have not prepared
> yourself to Merciful God unless you have performed sincerely the
> act of prayer.[9]

Khalil Gibran, an Americanized Lebanese, famous particularly
for his book *The Prophet,* wrote in the vein of al Ghazzali's
thinking. The same spirit moved both to address universal man,
and to address him with simplicity and sincerity.

Al Ghazzali's first contribution to Islam was to bring education
into an organic relation with a profound ethical system. He
taught that material gains could not bring happiness without a
moral and spiritual reawakening. Education must then not be
limited to the imparting of knowledge; it must stimulate the
moral consciousness of the individual.

---

[9] Al Ghazzali, *Ayyuha-L-Walad,* translated into French by Toufic
Sabbagh (Beyrouth Commission Internationale pour la traduction
des chefs-d'oeuvre, 1951), pp. 11-13.

His greatest contribution, however, was in the field of religion. His place in history rests on two achievements: (1) He was the leader in Islam's encounter with Greek philosophy. Owing to him, Islamic theology emerged victorious, and Arabic Neoplatonism died. (2) Through al Ghazzali, orthodoxy and mysticism were brought into closer contact and learned to tolerate one another, even to respect one another.

OMAR KHAYYAM

Omar Khayyam (died 1123) is widely and popularly known for his *Rubaiyat,* one of the most-translated books of world literature. He was, however, also a great mathematician and astronomer. He solved third- and fourth-degree equations by means of intersecting conics, the highest algebraic achievement of the Arabs, and the highest attained by modern mathematicians in the solution of equations of the fifth or higher degree by any universal method.

IBN TUFAIL

Ibn Tufail (died 1186) was secretary to several governors in Granada and finally a physician to the Sultan. Ibn Tufail's *Hayy ibn Yaqzan (The Living One, Son of the Vigilant),* is one of the most original books of the Middle Ages. Its main thought is that "human capacity unassisted by supernatural powers may attain the knowledge of the higher world and may by degrees find out its dependence upon a supreme being."[10]

Duncan B. MacDonald gives the following summary of *Hayy ibn Yaqzan.*

"He conceives two islands, the one inhabited and the other not. On the inhabited island we have conventional people living conventional lives, restrained by conventional religion of rewards and punishments. Two men there, Salaman and Asal (Absal),

---

[10] Watt, *op. cit.,* p. 15.

have raised themselves to a higher level of self-rule. Salaman adapts himself externally to the popular religion and rules the people. Asal, seeking to perfect himself still further in solitude, goes to the other island. But there he finds a man, Hayy ibn Yaqzan, who has lived alone from infancy and has gradually, by the innate and uncorrupted powers of his mind, developed to the highest level and reached the vision of the Divine. He has passed through all the stages of knowledge until the universe lies clear before him, and now he finds that his philosophy, thus reached, without prophet or revelation—and the purified religion of Asal, are one and the same. The story told by Asal of the people of the other island sitting in darkness stirs his soul, and he goes forth to them as a missionary. But he soon learns the method of Muhammad was the true one for the great masses, and that only by sensuous allegory and concrete things could they be reached and held. He retires to his island again to live the solitary life.[11]

This book was translated into Hebrew as early as the fourteenth century, into Latin and most European languages in the seventeenth century, into English in the eighteenth century, and into Russian in 1920 and Spanish in 1934.

IBN RUSHD

Ibn Rushd (died 1194), also known as Averroes, wrote commentaries on Aristotle, Plato, and al Farabi, and also a medical encyclopedia. Though famous as a physician, it was his fame as philosopher and commentator that endured.. His philosophy was in the tradition of Moslem Scholasticism and he ranked as the foremost expounder of Aristotle. Ibn Rushd's work was essentially a reaction against al Ghazzali's mysticism. The work for which he was best known in Islam is the refutation of al Ghazzali's *Incoherence of Philosophy* by his *Incoherence of Incoherence*. His commentaries, however, made considerably more stir, particularly among Christians and Jews, than did this refu-

---

[11] Duncan B. MacDonald, *Development of Muslim Theology* (New York, Scribner's, 1903), p. 367.

tation. Ibn Rushd's religious writings were to some extent compatible with Jewish beliefs but not with Moslem, and still less, Christian doctrine. He upheld the Aristotelian notion of the eternity of the world, which denies the dogma of its creation.

Ibn Rushd represents a modification of the positions of al Farabi and ibn Sina with regard to the concept of the intellect. Man, ibn Sina stated and ibn Rushd agreed, possesses two kinds of intellect, active and passive. The former is stimulated to action by the operation of the agent intellect and thus becomes acquired intellect. The individual intellects are many, but the agent intellect is one, though present in each individual intellect, just as the one sun is active in each body it illuminates. Ibn Rushd differed from ibn Sina with regard to the passive intellect, the seat of latent faculties upon which the agent operates. In all earlier systems, this passive intellect was regarded as purely individual and as operated on by the emanation of the universal agent, but ibn Rushd regarded the passive intellect as only a portion of a universal soul, individual only insofar as it temporarily occupies an individual body. He saw even the passive powers as parts of a universal force animating the whole of nature.

The Christian Scholastics interpreted ibn Rushd's views to mean that there can be no real ego in any individual if the conscious life of each is a part of the conscious life of a universal soul. They claimed, therefore, that ibn Rushd was subversive of individuality. They also argued that ibn Rushd's views denied the immortality of the soul and therefore were not compatible with Christian principles.

Ibn Rushd's view on religion and the common man is noteworthy. He divided men into three classes, the highest, the intermediate, and the lowest. The highest includes those whose religious beliefs are based on what in philosophical terms is called demonstration, the result of reasoning from syllogisms which are a priori certain; these are the men to whom the philosopher makes his appeal. The intermediate are those who have not attained the use of pure reason or intuition, but are capable of carrying on a discussion by means of which their faith can be defended and argued for. One should not use demonstration with this class, but it is right to enter into argument with them and to assist them to rise above the level of those whose belief is based on authority. The lowest contains those whose faith is based on authority of a teacher or on a presumption that is not based on the exercise of reason and that therefore cannot be argued out. It is wrong to put demonstration or reason before people of this type, for it can only cause them doubt and difficulty.

This is the common theory of twofold truth—the one, more profound, for the philosophers and those philosophical in nature; the other, simple, for the masses. In other words, one should teach people according to their ability to comprehend. One cannot teach all people in the same way, and any attempt at teaching the reconciliation of religion with philosophy, or of faith with reason, in only one way, leads to an implicit, if not explicit, acknowledgment of a twofold truth.

Ibn Rushd's views, through many translations, deeply influenced Jewish philosophy and the translators, his disciples, introduced him to Latin Christendom. Jewish Averroism reached its zenith under Levi ben Gershon in the fourteenth century and continued vigorously until the end of the fifteenth century. Levi ben Gershon's most important work as representative and philosopher of medieval Judaism may well have been his commentaries on the commentaries of ibn Rushd.

Christian scholars were as deeply influenced as Jewish scholars. Ibn Rushd's commentaries had caused revulsions among the Moslems of Spain, among the Talmudists, and finally in Christendom. Aristotle and ibn Rushd reached Christian scholars at about the same time; and they were at first treated as the same evil: in 1210 both were forbidden by a provincial council at Paris; in 1215 the prohibition was confirmed with special reference to the *Metaphysics* of ibn Rushd; in 1231 the Pope prohibited the reading of their works unless they were completely expurgated. (In the meantime, Averroism, being ostracized, became more subversive.) In 1277 the Bishop of Paris condemned specifically 219 errors in the teachings of Averroes and Aristotle. Thus ibn Rushd came to be regarded as the archinfidel and the greatest enemy of the Christian faith. Aquinas' immense efforts against him were indicative of the general reaction against Averroism. Notwithstanding the Church's opposition, Averroes' writings remained alive in Europe until the sixteenth century. In the *Inferno,* Dante wrote about ibn Rushd as "Averroes che'l gran comento feo" (who wrote the great commentary [on Aristotle]), acknowledging his preeminence. In the nineteenth century, Ernest Renan wrote much about ibn Rushd, and William James's *Principles of Psychology* supports some of ibn Rushd's views.

CHAPTER FOUR

Ibn Arabi

Ibn Arabi, the mystic philosopher who flourished in the thirteenth century, is best known for the following works:

Kitab al Futuhat al Makkiya (The Revelation of Mecca), a treatise on mysticism, including an allegory of the ascension of man to heaven;

Kitab al Isra Ila Maqam al Asra (The Nocturnal Journey toward the Station of the Most Magnanimous), dealing with the same theme;

Kitab Tarjuman al Ashwaq, love poems and his interpretation of them;

Kitab Dhakhair al-a-Laq (The Treasures of the Devoted);

Fusus-ul-Hikma (Gems of Philosophy, or Bezels of Divine Wisdom).

The appearance of Arabic literary themes in medieval Europe evidenced a general trend. Together with the fruits of Arabic scholarship translated into Latin, Arab narrative literature fertilized the nascent literature of Europe. Not only did Dante derive some of his cosmogony from Arab sources, but also Boccaccio in the *Decameron* and Chaucer in the "*Squire's Tale*" of *The Canterbury Tales* echoed Arab stories.

Ibn Arabi's love poem *The Treasures of the Devoted* certainly shows kinship with the *dolce stil nuovo*, Dante's *Convivio*, and the tale of the meeting of Beatrice and Dante, an episode unprecedented in Christian legend and foreign to the spirit of

Christianity. Ibn Arabi also had a Beatrice—Nizam—and because of a scandal caused by his odes, he wrote a commentary to clear her. Similarly, in the *Convivio,* Dante shows why his love songs for Beatrice had been interpreted as dealing with sensual rather than spiritual love.

It is possible that the great scheme of Dante's poem, as well as many details of it, were suggested to him (indirectly, of course, for he did not know Arabic) by Moslem models. Miguel Asim Palacios, an authority on the subject, has pointed out that many peculiar features of ibn Arabi's description of Hell, Paradise, and the Beatific Vision are reproduced in Dante's poem with a closeness that can scarcely be fortuitous.[1] With regard to the Prophet's miraculous journey, ibn Arabi's work related the three cycles of Moslem tradition.

1. The *Isra,* that is, his visit to heaven, or according to later and more popular interpretation, his night journey to Jerusalem;

2. The *Miraj,* his ascension to heaven, an event celebrated every year by the festival Dar al Islam;

3. A combination of the *Isra* and *Miraj,* which constitutes a complete model of Dante's visits to Hell, Purgatory, and Paradise.

Asim Palacios, R. A. Nicholson, and others believe that the parallelism is such that only one conclusion is justified, namely, that the *Miraj* and other religious legends must have passed into the common stock of literary themes that was accessible to the best minds in thirteenth-century Europe.

In view of the foregoing, Paget Toynbee's work [2] on Dante should be extended and critically investigated for further clues as to the extent of the influence of al Farghani and ibn Arabi on Dante.

---

[1] Miguel Asim Palacios, *Islam and the Divine Comedy* (London, John Murray, 1926).

[2] Paget Toynbee, *Dante Studies and Research* (London, Methuen, 1902).

Professor Hitti has commented that Raymond Lull and other Christian mystics bear traces of ibn Arabi's influence.[3] R. A. Nicholson [4] suggests also that much in ibn Arabi's work is echoed by Spinoza, and he declares, along with Hitti, that ibn Arabi influenced some of the Scholastics, not only Lull, but also Duns Scotus, Alexander Hales, Roger Bacon and others.

The Revelation of Mecca is ibn Arabi's magnum opus. The author claimed that he was commanded by the Prophet to write this book, that on one occasion he met a youth (symbolizing a celestial spirit) who revealed to him the esoteric Temple hidden from profane eyes, commanded him to record the mysteries that would be revealed to him, and breathed into him the comprehension of all things. Understanding came to him gradually through a succession of different visions. Some were obtained through an ascension to heaven, an ascension repeated in its general plan and in numerous details in *The Divine Comedy.* Ibn Arabi's ascension proceeded through seven stages corresponding to the astronomical heavens from the moon to Saturn. In each stage he met prophets who revealed to him a certain set of mysteries.

In the first stage, or heaven, that of the moon, Adam instructed him on the significance of the divine names, on changes in the material elements, and on the generation of all living things, including man. The second heaven was that of Mercury, in which Jesus and John revealed secrets about the performance of miracles. In subsequent heavens, prophets from Joseph and Enoch to Moses and Abraham instructed him in subjects ranging from causes of night and day to the life hereafter.

In the second part of the ascension, ibn Arabi reached the four mystic rivers representing the Pentateuch, the Book of Psalms, the Gospel, and the *Quran.* He then penetrated to the

---

[3] Philip K. Hitti, *History of Syria* (New York, Macmillan, 1951), p. 625.

[4] Nicholson, *op. cit.,* p. 228.

sphere of the fixed stars in which dwelt the angelic spirits. After crossing the zodiac, he reached the stool upon which rest the feet of God, symbols of His justic and mercy. Here he learned the many mysteries of the cosmos and, finally, beheld the utmost secret of the divine essence.

The themes of ibn Arabi's philosophy of mysticism are many and complex. Underlying them is the idea of God who is everything. Ibn Arabi's God is not one who creates or from whom anything but Himself emanates, but a God who manifests Himself in an infinity of forms. While the *Quran* declares, "There is but one God," ibn Arabi maintained that there is nothing *but* God. While the Islamic God is the creator and cause of the universe, ibn Arabi's God is everything. This shift suggests a step from monotheism to pantheism. The finite God of religion is distinguished from the infinite God of mysticism in ibn Arabi's philosophy. The God of religion reveals Himself in various forms, reflected in the different religions. It depends upon the comprehension of the believer which one of these forms (religions) he accepts. The God of the mystic contains all His forms, for the mystic's heart alone is receptive.

CHAPTER FIVE

Ibn Khaldun

Ibn Khaldun (1332-1406) gained distinction as scholar, courtier, and administrator, but his fame rests on his monumental *Kitab al Ibar wa Diwan al Mubtada wal Khabar fi Ayyam al Arab wal Ajam wal Berber wa man Asarahum min Dhiwai-l-Sultan al Akbar (Instructive Examples and Collection of Origins and Information Concerning the History of the Arabs, Persians, and Berbers),* a universal history, and the theory of history he set forth in his prolegomena to it, the *Muqaddama.*

Ibn Khaldun's family had emigrated from South Arabia to Spain in the eighth century during the early years of the Moslem conquest. The family settled within the triangle formed by Cordova, Seville, and Granada, where they soon attained political prominence. When Seville fell to invading forces (1248), the Khalduns moved on to Northwest Africa, where refugees from Spain settled in ever-growing numbers. For several decades members of the Khaldun family held high positions in the government of Northwest Africa.

In ibn Khaldun's time, the political situation was very unstable, and he moved from city to city in search of his fortune. His family connections, personal friendships, and intellectual gifts gave him entree to some administrative and political positions but also led to one term of imprisonment and a few near arrests. He finally abandoned politics and lived out his days in Cairo.

Ibn Khaldun began his history of the world while he was under the protection of an Arab tribe in Oran. He was also the author of various other works, but the *Kitab al Ibar* remains his monument.

The book is divided into three parts:

1. The *Muqaddama* (the *Prolegomena*, a philosophical introduction);

2. History of the Arabs, and the Nabateans, Syrians, Persians, Jews, Copts, Greeks, Romans, Turks, Franks;

3. History of the Berbers and of the Moslem dynasties of North Africa.

The *Muqaddama* has been declared by all scholars in the field to be far more important than Parts 2 and 3, yet it is doubtful whether sufficient study has been made of these parts, owing to the lack of translations from the Arabic. The *Muqaddama* itself was finally translated into English in 1957. Prior to that time, only sectional translations into English existed. The first complete translation of the *Muqaddama* into any other language was a Turkish version of 1730; a complete French translation was published in 1862-1865.

The *Muqaddama* is made up of six sections preceded by a long introduction which includes significant information on historiography, an appreciation of the various approaches to history, a glimpse at the different kinds of errors to which historians are prone, and some suggestions as to the causes of these errors.

The first section deals with society in general, its various kinds, its geographical distribution, and the portion of the earth that is civilized. The second takes up nomadic societies, including savage tribes. The third is a discourse on states—dynasties, the caliphates, the spiritual and temporal powers, and political ranks. The fourth section discusses non-nomadic societies, cities and provinces; the fifth deals with crafts, ways of making a living, and other economic activities; and the sixth with the various classifications of sciences, and methods of learning and teaching.

An attempt will be made here to note for each section those of ibn Khaldun's ideas considered most significant by present-day authorities.

MAN AND SOCIETY

Man cannot survive alone; human society is essential to him. Cooperation occupies a key position in ibn Khaldun's thinking, as making possible man's survival and the existence of society. Did man himself resolve all this? Ibn Khaldun did not think so. Man, he believed, is social and political by nature. God's will is to have social organization, and He created man in such a way that he would seek to build and succeed in building a civiliza-zation. Mutual cooperation is the mechanism by which God's will is fulfilled.

Asabiyya, OR SOCIAL SOLIDARITY

Ibn Khaldun discerned in the life of nations two dominant forces that mold their destiny. The primitive and cardinal force ibn Khaldun called *asabiyya,* or binding elements in society, the social solidarity or group feeling that unites people, a nation, and an empire and that in its widest scope is equivalent to patriotism; however, patriotism and *asabiyya* are not synonymous. Even in its most extreme form, patriotism is but a shadow of *asabiyya* as described by ibn Khaldun. *Asabiyya* originates and flourishes where the instinct of self-preservation awakens a keen sense of kinship and drives men to make common cause with each other. It is the vital energy of the states; by it they rise and grow; as it weakens, they decline.

The second force is religion; it produces that solidarity without which no state can exist. It is secondary to *asabiyya* and actually serves to bolster the latter. With this religious force, the Arabs had become capable of founding a great civilization.

Religious organization doubles the strength of group feeling. The impact on other civilizations of religion combined with *asabiyya* (Islam and group feeling) was tremendous.

What are the bases of these two great uniting forces?

Asabiyya results from blood relationship and the ties that grow out of it. Blood ties lead to a bond of affection for one's relatives and to the obligation to extend help to them and protect them from harm. If the direct relationship between blood relatives is very close and the contact between them is frequent, the ties are strong and clearly lead to a feeling of solidarity. If, however, the relationship is distant or if the relationship is close, but the individuals do not meet frequently, such feelings will weaken. But some remaining vestige leads to a feeling of solidarity in time of need. Also, if one does not help his relatives, adverse criticism makes itself felt. Thus, social pressure strengthens solidarity.

Corresponding to blood relationship in generating group feeling are companionship, living together, long acquaintance or friendship, sharing foster-parents, and being together in various circumstances of life. Such ties lead to affection, cooperation, and mutual help.

Religion generates group feeling because it does away with jealousy and envy felt by members of the group toward each other and turns their faces to the truth. Once their eyes have seen the truth, they will all have the same outlook and the same objectives, and they will be willing to fight and even die for these objectives, while those who lack worthy goals and deep convictions fall in time of war before the dedicated believers. In fact, that is what happened during the early conquests of Islam. Though Islam was outnumbered many times, its group feeling and deep faith enabled it to score decisive victories.

In summary, *asabiyya,* the binding element in society results from (1) blood relationship, (2) religion, and (3) such other facts as living together, companionship, prolonged acquaintance or friendship, growing up together, and the like. The strength and weakness of a nation is largely determined by the strength and weakness of *asabiyya.*

Sati Bey el Husry has claimed that the entire six books of the

Prolegomena belong to the field of sociology. Charles Issawi agrees, and adds that ibn Khaldun was the first to state clearly some of the basic principles of sociology:

1. Social phenomena appear to obey laws that, while not so absolute as those governing natural phenomena, are sufficiently constant to cause social events generally to follow regular patterns and sequences. A grasp of these laws enables the sociologist to anticipate the trend of events.

2. These laws cannot be significantly influenced by any individual.

3. These laws can be discovered only by gathering facts and observing concomitants and sequences. Facts can be gathered only from the records of past events and from observation of present events. Explanation of phenomena consists in relating the correlations thus observed to accepted principles of psychology, biology, and other disciplines.

4. The same social laws operate in societies with the same kind of structure.

5. Societies are not static; they change, and their change is due to innumerable causes, in particular to the contact between different peoples and classes and the consequent imitations that take place.

This "principle of imitation" defined by ibn Khaldun foreshadowed the thinking of Thorstein Veblen .

Ibn Khaldun's observations on settled life as compared to nomadic life are full of sociological insights:

Settled people make their living from crafts and commerce and have less mobility than those who live in the country. City life is a life of relative comfort; it is thus "soft" compared to the "tough" life in the country. The nomadic (country) life is led by people who make their living from agriculture and animal husbandry, earning only enough to meet their bare necessities. The objective therefore is to settle in the city.

Man must be governed by qualified leaders; if these are just and the laws not oppressive, the people will make use of their abilities, and develop them to their full potential. By the same token restrictive laws weaken souls and destroy energy and fortitude. To ibn Khaldun, the best government is the one that governs least. Under such government, man will rely on himself for his needs. This is the character of the nomadic desert life; it is the good life. Sedentary people become used to the comparatively easy life and accustomed to luxuries. Thus these habits and customs replace the natural disposition of man and make for an "artificial life"; only desert life is the natural life.

GROWTH AND DECLINE OF SOCIAL ORGANIZATIONS

Ibn Khaldun sought universal laws which may explain the rise and fall of civilizations, and came to the following conclusions:

Esprit de corps *(asabiyya)* is manifestly the strongest psychological bond of all political communities, especially among nomadic peoples in their original state, and made such peoples formidable empire builders. But, *asabiyya* must also be accompanied by religion as a prerequisite to the building of an empire. *Asabiyya*, however, weakened and finally disappeared as nomadic life came to an end.

The growth of a civilization depends upon a sedentary life and the rule of law and order. The Arabs, according to ibn Khaldun, did not qualify as builders of civilizations as long as they lived in the desert and had to lead a nomadic life. They were fierce, freedom-loving people and did not easily submit to authority.

As the Arabs left nomadic life behind they rapidly developed a noteworthy civilization, in which religion had a significant part. It was Islam that supplied the restraining influence, so that bellicosity and pride, envy, jealousy, and rash ambition lost their virulence. Islam did indeed bring out the best in the Arabs.

In ibn Khaldun's time, however, there were already ominous signs of a decline of Islam. They led him to the conclusion that in the life of states and dynasties, similarly to that of individuals, there is a period of progress followed by a period of decline and finally of extinction. Ibn Khaldun may thus be considered a forerunner of Oswald Spengler.

In comparing people and states, ibn Khaldun set forth the existence of a definite cycle. According to him, nobility and prestige in a family reach their end in four generations. The first generation is that of the builder of the power; his recollections of the difficulties he encountered are vivid and therefore he guards his position with all his strength. While the son acquires his father's attitudes they are reduced in vigor, as they are based on learning from others rather than on their having been initiated by him. The men of the third generation rely upon tradition and imitation. They do not match those who exercise independent judgment. The fourth generation loses all the qualities that could preserve prestige. The men of this generation assume that prestige belongs to them by descent and keep aloof from those whose group feeling they should share.

So, too, kingdoms are born, attain maturity, and die within a definite period rarely exceeding three generations, or a total of 120 years. The first generation of a dynasty retains the desert qualities of toughness, independence, and aggressiveness. Its members have a strong group feeling. They share each other's problems and fortunes; the second generation becomes less close to the people, emphasizing their royal authority. Its members, says ibn Khaldun, thus change from nomadic to sedentary life, from hardship to luxury, from solidarity to rivalry. Many of the old virtues of desert life, however, remain because the people have had direct contact with the first generation. The people of this generation live in the hope that the conditions that existed in the first generation will one day return, or they live under the illusion that the old conditions still exist.

The third generation becomes completely oblivious of the desert life. It has lost its social solidarity and even its love of power and must now be ruled by force. The people of this generation seek luxury and become accustomed to it; they become lazy and must be protected like women and children. The government is compelled to hire soldiers for their protection. Within three generations the kingdom has degenerated to such an extent that its final destruction is not far off.

According to ibn Khaldun, a state is limited to five stages:

1. The fight for supremacy and the seizure of power. Group solidarity is at its peak during this stage. The ruler claims nothing for himself exclusively and this furthers social solidarity.

2. The establishment of sovereignty and in consequence the weakening of solidarity.

3. The leisure and tranquillity of established rule.

4. The ruler imitating his predecessor's way in all matters.

5. Extravagance and luxury prevail and uninhibited indulgence in desires of every kind. Corruption of the army—increasing of taxes that cannot be collected—and finally, the destruction of the dynasty.

After a state has had its period of glory, it approaches its decay marked by various signs: the growth of factions, for a country with many sects and factions has less central authority; the growth of luxury, for when the ruler has stabilized his power he turns to the enjoyment of the yield of the state; he becomes incapable of directing the affairs of the government because he lacks courage or contents himself with wasting his time in varieties of pleasures and luxuries.

Since the *Muqaddama* consists largely of psychological, sociological, and economic abstractions and their elucidation, it is difficult to allocate certain parts of it to any particular field. Much of the fourth and fifth sections deals with economics *per se,* but abbreviated "theories," or "principles," also appear in other sections.

Ibn Khaldun was the first thinker to treat economics as a special discipline outside the fields of ethics and philosophy. Earlier writers concerned with economics such as al Farabi, ibn Sina, ibn Rushd, and al Ghazzali discussed basic economic concepts in order to reach equitable solutions to the problems of taxes, interests on money lent, the legitimacy of sources of income, the right of inheritance, and just wages and prices.

Ibn Khaldun, essentially a liberal, rejected all restrictions on economic freedom. He saw labor as the main cause of wealth and praised manual labor at a time when most people despised it, but he condemned slavery and slave labor. He believed that the value of a commodity is determined by the labor embodied in it.

Production, not trade, as the mercantilists believed, is the source of wealth. Gold and silver, actually not of greater utility than iron, are prized because of their scarcity. Long before Locke and Hume, ibn Khaldun stated that each country must obtain the gold it needs through foreign trade.

He believed in competition and strongly condemned monopoly. Therefore, he considered the increase of population and infrequency of excessive wealth a blessing. In his view the economic sphere should not disregard moral and spiritual values.

Private property and lower taxes are incentives to increased production.

With regard to politics and economics he set forth these beliefs on their interaction:

The functions of the state are simply to guarantee security, peace, and equity in transactions. The state may also spend money on such social services as care of the poor, widows and orphans, and the blind. The state may also pay special pensions and build and staff hospitals. Additional regulations are an encroachment upon the freedom of the individual and are an evil. The approved state functions give the government the right to levy taxes. It is the duty of the state to levy taxes in a fair manner; no preference or special exemptions should be given on the basis of rank or wealth, and taxes should be levied according to the individual's ability to pay.

Again, ibn Khaldun was convinced that a light tax burden encourages individuals to enter business, thereby increasing the total yield of taxation. The lighter the tax burden, the greater the incentive.

The wise government does not hoard wealth but spends its income to improve the conditions of its citizens and the country. The prosperity of the nation depends upon the expenditure of the government. The country is prosperous if the government spends all it collects in taxes. Income under this condition continues to circulate between the government and its citizens. The state may reduce the incentive to work and to produce by imposing undue burdens on its citizens. Such measures are extremely harmful because they lead to a slackening in enterprise, and this is in proportion to the measures' oppressiveness.

The first stage of economic development includes those occupations that deal with the bare necessities of life. As soon as the people engaged in these occupations enjoy more than the bare necessities, they desire more leisure and will be eager to obtain luxuries. Habits of luxury in food, clothing, and living quarters will be formed; crafts will develop and reach ever greater height. In this stage people make their living in manufacture and trade.

The basic means of making a livelihood are agriculture, crafts, and trade—agriculture ranking first and requiring little schooling. Crafts and trade represent a higher stage of man's development and call for more learning and more preparation. Gold, silver, and precious stones are minerals and have exchange value like other minerals. Society, acting through human labor, brings gold and silver to light by mining and increases or decreases their quantity.

CONCLUSION

The scope of the *Prolegomena* is encyclopedic. The emphasis is on the sociological, political, and economic fields. Ibn Khaldun contrasted nomadic life and sedentary life and considered sedentary life the one condition of cultural progress, but also the source of corruption and decadence, the origin at once of urbanity and of degeneration. He mildly opposed the nomadic life because it rejected almost any kind of law and order, but he loved the independence and the freedom it provided.

In his views the duties of the state were simply to guarantee security, peace, and equity in transactions. Ibn Khaldun wrote about the sovereignty of the ruler, the meaning of the caliphate, and about the different theories on monarchy. In short, he laid down the qualities and duties of the ideal prince or ruler. He also dealt with the defense of the state, the devotion of the soldiery, the competition in business of the prince with his people and the encroachment of the government upon private property. Machiavelli treated of many of these subjects in *The Prince* or in *History of Florence,* but Machiavelli studied the prince from a purely pragmatical point of view. He drew his conclusions from success achieved or failure suffered, without any consideration of moral principles. Ibn Khaldun's treatment of his subject is broader and his conclusions more idealistic; his main concerns were with the causes of the rise and fall of civilizations rather than the power-motivated policy of the prince.

Among the many good qualities a prince should have, ibn Khaldun listed the following: desire for goodness, generosity, tolerance, hospitality, a sense of obligation to support dependents and indigents, equanimity in adverse circumstances, liberality with money for the preservation of honor, respect for the religious law and for the scholars learned in it, fairness and compassion for those too weak to take care of themselves, humility toward the poor and attentiveness to the complaints of supplicants.

Modern scholars have paid tribute to ibn Khaldun's breadth of vision. Arnold Toynbee wrote:

> Ibn Khaldun . . . achieved in a single acquiescence of less than four years length out of a fifty-four years' span of adult working life, a life-work in the shape of a piece of literature which can bear comparison with the work of Thucydides or the work of a Machiavelli for both breadth and profundity of vision as well as

for sheer intellectual power. Ibn Khaldun's star shines the more brightly by contrast with the foil of darkness against which it flashes out; for while Thucydides and Machiavelli and Clarendon are all brilliant representatives of brilliant times and places, Ibn Khaldun is the sole point of light in his quarter of the firmament. He is indeed the one outstanding personality in the history of a civilization whose social life on the whole was solitary, poor, nasty, brutish and short. In his chosen field of intellectual activity he appears to have been inspired by no predecessors and to have no kindred souls among his contemporaries and to have kindled no answering spark of inspiration in any successors; and yet, in the *Prolegomena* to his Universal History he has conceived and formulated a philosophy of history which is undoubtedly the greatest work of its kind that has ever yet been created by any mind in any time or place. It was his single brief acquiescence from a life of practical activity that gave Ibn Khaldun his opportunity to cast his creative thought into literary shape.[1]

Ibn Khaldun's translator, Franz Rosenthal, commented as follows:

At the beginning of the nineteenth century, European scholars joined with the Turks in studying Ibn Khaldun. Many ideas discussed in European West long after Ibn Khaldun's time were found, amazingly enough, not to be as new as he had been thought, but to have been known, in their rudiments at least, to the northwest African of the fourteenth century who founded a "new science" in the Maqaddama. Moreover, Ibn Khaldun has been claimed as a forerunner to or compared with Machiavelli, Bodin, Vico, Gibbon, Gobineau, Tarde, Breysing, W. James and Hegel.[2]

---

[1] Arnold J. Toynbee, *A Study of History* (New York, Oxford University Press, 1934-1954), Vol. III, pp. 321-322.

[2] Franz Rosenthal, in ibn Khaldun, *The Muqaddimah, an Introduction to History*, translated by Franz Rosenthal (New York, Pantheon, 1958), Vol. I, p. lxviii.

CHAPTER SIX

Translations into Arabic, A.D. 650-1000

After A.D. 1100, civilization began to shift westward; by 1400 the shift was complete, and it has never reversed itself. This shift came about largely by the assimilation of the East by the West. The Arabs, roughly the people of Islam, had received much from the Greeks and the Hindus; they added greatly to this cultural treasury in the four hundred or more years of their ascendancy. Greco-Hindu-Arabic knowledge was at first transferred slowly but later poured from the Arabic vessels into Latin and Hebrew ones.

Jewish scholars, mostly by way of Spain, were one main factor of the shift to the West. Christian scholars, especially translators from Arabic into Latin, were another. Just as the acquisition of Greek knowledge moved the Arab world to leadership in the field of learning, so the West probed in the dark until it found in Arabic manuscripts the learning of the Greeks. These cultural transmissions were largely the work of translators. The activities of these translators into and from Arabic were of paramount importance.

The following survey indicates the wealth of knowledge made part of Islamic learning.

THE PERIOD A.D. 650-800

SEVERUS SEBOKHT, bishop of the convent of Qen-neshrē on the Upper Euphrates which flourished about A.D. 650, was a scientist and philosopher. Under his leadership the monastery became one of the main centers of Greek learning. Much of the Greek and perhaps Hindu knowledge was transmitted to the Arabic-speaking peoples through his efforts. He had the belief, unusual for his time and even for the present time, that scientific progress must proceed on an international basis.

KHALID IBN YAZID IBN MURAWIYA, an Umayyad prince and philosopher, is said to have encouraged Greek philosophers in Egypt to translate Greek books into Arabic. These were probably the first translations made in Islam. Ibn Yazid lived in Egypt and died sometime between A.D. 704 and 708.

Muhammad, son of Ibrahim al Fazari, translated into Arabic, in about A.D. 772, the Sanskrit astronomical work *Siddhantä*. His father is said to have been the first Moslem to construct astrolabes, and Muhammad is believed to have been one of the first scholars mentioned in connection with Hindu mathematics. His translations may have carried Hindu numerals to Islam.

Abu Sahl al Fadl ibn Naubkht, a Persian and chief librarian to Harun al Rashid, translated astronomical works from Persian into Arabic.

Jirjis ibn Jibril ibn Bakhtyashu, a Nestorian Persian, was the first to translate medical works into Arabic; he was also the first of an illustrious Nestorian family of physicians attached to a long series of Abbasid caliphs. They all exerted a strong influence upon Moslem medicine in the eighth and ninth centuries. Bakhtyashu came to Baghdad from Jundishapur, where he had been, at the behest of Caliph al Mansur, in charge of a hospital.

Abu Yahya ibn al Batriq, a physician who lived in the eighth century was, like Bakhtyashu, employed by Caliph al Mansur. He translated from Greek into Arabic some of the works of Hippocrates and Galen, Ptolemy's *Quadripartitum* and probably the *Almagest*, Ptolemy's great astronomical work.

Abdallah ibn al Muqaffa (executed about A.D. 758) was of

Persian origin and flourished in Basra. He translated from Pah-
lawi several treatises dealing with logic and medicine. He is
chiefly known, however, for the translation of *Siyar Muluk al-
Ajam (The History of the Kings of Persia)* and *Kalila Wa Dimna
(The Fables of the Five Books)*.

Al Mansur, the second Abbasid Caliph (754 to his death in
775), a founder of Baghdad, is memorable because of the many
translations made during his reign from the Syriac, Persian,
Greek, and Hindu languages.

Harun al Rashid, fifth and one of the greatest Abbasid mon-
archs, ruled from 786 to his death in 809; he was a munificent
patron of science, art, and literature and continued the Abbasid
tradition of having Greek works translated.

THE PERIOD A.D. *800-900*

Al Mamun of Baghdad (A.D. 786-833), the seventh and probably the greatest Abbasid caliph (813-833), was an even more
lavish patron of science and letters than Harun al Rashid. He
made it his life's goal to obtain and translate Greek manuscripts
and even sent a mission to the Byzantine Emperor Leon of Ar-
menia to that purpose. Al Mamun invited, housed, and supported
Jewish and Christian scholars to translate these manuscripts into
Arabic. He also founded Bayt al Hikma (House of Wisdom), an
academy of science and built an observatory on the plain of
Palmyra. During his reign hundreds of manuscripts were translated from Greek into Arabic.

Abu Zakariya Yahya ibn Batriq translated into Arabic Plato's
Timaeos, Hippocrates' books on the signs of death, various works
of Aristotle, Galen's *De Theriaca* and *Pisonem,* and probably
Secretum Secretorum.

Al Kindi, philosopher in his own right, translated and directed
the translation of many Greek works into Arabic. The most
famous of his translations was a Neoplatonic treatise based on
Books IV through VI of the *Enneads* of Plotinus.

Jibrail ibn Bakhtyashu, grandson of the earlier translator of the same name, served as physician to both al Mamun and Harun al Rashid and translated many Greek medical manuscripts.

Abd al Masih Naima of Hims translated, in about A.D. 835, some Neoplatonic writings that were erroneously taken to be "the ethics of Aristotle." This work was later improved upon by al Kindi.

Sahl al Tabari, a Jewish astronomer and physician, was one of the first translators of Ptolemy's *Almagest* into Arabic.

Ibn Sahda translated many medical works from Greek into Syriac and into Arabic. He is credited with the translation of some of Hippocrates' work into Arabic and also some of Galen's.

Al Hajjaj ibn Yusuf ibn Matar was the first translator into Arabic of Euclid's *Elements*. He was also one of the first translators of the *Almagest* into Arabic, working from a Syriac version in about A.D. 830.

Thabit ibn Qurra (A.D. 829-901) was a physician, mathematician, astronomer, and one of the great translators from Greek into Syriac and Arabic. He founded a school of translators of which many of his own family were members. Translated by him or under his direction were Books V-VII of Apollonius of Perga, several works by Archimedes, the writings of Euclid, Theodosius, Galen, Eutocios, and Ptolemy's *Geography*. He also revised earlier translations.

Al Baladhuri, who flourished at the court of the Caliph al Mutawakkil, translated several works from Persian into Arabic.

The three brothers Banu Musa, each a specialist in one or more of the sciences, devoted most of their time and wealth to the acquisition of Greek manuscripts and their translation into Arabic. Hunain ibn Ishaq and Thabit ibn Qurra were the most famous translators they employed. Many mathematical, mechanical, and astronomical treatises and some logical works were translated for them.

Abu Zakariya Yuhanna ibn Masawaih, a physician who trans-

lated various Greek medical works into Arabic, was the first to
head the *House of Wisdom* established by al Mamun.

Hunain ibn Ishaq (A.D. 808-877) was a Nestorian physician,
one of the greatest scholars of his time and an outstanding translator. He studied in Baghdad under Yahya ibn Masawaih, the
director of the *House of Wisdom*, and at medical schools in
Alexandria and other cities. He returned to head the school,
equipped not only with the best medical knowledge available
at that time but also with a remarkable knowledge of Greek.
Hunain traveled far in search of authoritative manuscripts of
Greek medical texts. He collated them, examined the existing
Syriac and Arabic versions, and translated some of them over
again. Later he revised some of his earlier works. To appreciate
his efforts more fully, one must realize that earlier Syriac translations of Greek medical works were unsatisfactory and the
Arabic versions, now twice removed from the original, were no
better. Hunain carefully compared these versions and prepared
his own translation. His translations included as many as ninety-
five Syriac versions, five of them revisions, and thirty-nine Arabic
versions of various books by Galen and others. Hunain would
translate from Greek into Syriac; one of his translators would
translate the Syriac into Arabic, and Hunain would then revise
the final text. He worked as a translator for over fifty years. The
number and quality of medical translations made by Hunain and
his school were the foundation of that Moslem knowledge which
dominated medical thought until the seventeenth century.

Ishaq ibn Hunain, son of Hunain, physician and mathematician, was one of the ablest translators who worked in Hunain's
school of translation. The following translations are ascribed to
him: Arabic versions of the *Sophist* of Plato, the *Metaphysics*,
De Anima, De Generatione et De Corruptione, as well as commentaries of Porphyry, Alexander of Aphrodisias, and Ammonius.
He also translated Euclid, Ptolemy's *Almagest*, Menelaos, Archimedes, Autolycus, Hypsicles, the pseudo-Aristotelian *De Plantis*,
two Galenic works into Syriac and ten into Arabic.

Qusta ibn Luqa was a physician, astronomer, mathematician, philosopher, and translator. The translations of Diophantus, Theodosius, Autolycus, Hypsicles, Aristarchus, and Heron were made or revised by him or translated under his direction. He also revised some of Ishaq ibn Hunain's work.

Hubaish ibn al Hasan, physician, nephew of Hunain ibn Ishaq and his collaborator in the translation of Greek works into Syriac and into Arabic, is given credit for translating Galenic works into Syriac and into Arabic.

Isa ibn Yahya, a disciple of Hunain, translated various Galenic works into Syriac and into Arabic. He also translated some of the writings of Oribasius, who was the author of a philosophical encyclopedia.

Yusuf al Khuri, physician and mathematician, lived during the caliphate of al Muqtafi and translated from Syriac into Arabic. He translated Archimedes' lost work on the triangles and Galen's *De Simplicium Temperamentis et Facultatibus*.

Ayyub al Ruhawi was one of the main translators of medical works from Greek into Syriac. Hunain ibn Ishaq ascribed to him the translation of thirty-five Galenic works.

Salmawaih ibn Bunan helped Hunain ibn Ishaq to translate Galen's *Methodus medendi*.

Stephanos, son of Basilios, was a close associate and a collaborator of Hunain ibn Ishaq; according to Hunain, he translated nine Galenic works into Arabic. He was the first to translate Dioscorides into Arabic and the first Arabic version of Oribasius is ascribed to him..

Musa ibn Khalid was an important member of Hunain's school of translators. He translated into Arabic several books of Galen's works from Hunain's Syriac version.

THE PERIOD A.D. *900-1000*

Matta ibn Yunus rendered into Arabic the *Analytica Posterior* and the *Poetics* of Aristotle, Alexander's of Aphrodisias commentary on *De generatione et De corruptione* and Themistios' commentary on Book 30 of the *Metaphysics*, all from existing Syriac versions. He was al Farabi's teacher.

Yahya ibn Adi studied under ibn Yunus and al Farabi; he revised Matta's translation of Themistios' commentary on Aristotle's *De Coelo* and translated the commentary of Alexander of Aphrodisias on Aristotle's *Meteorology.*

Abu Uthman al Dimishqi flourished under the Caliph al Muqtadir. He was a physician, a mathematician, and a translator. He translated into Arabic works of Aristotle, Galen, Porphyry, and Euclid. His most important translation was that of Book X of Euclid together with Pappus' commentary on it, which is extant only in Arabic.

Al Hakam II, or ibn Abd al Rahman III; called also al Mustansir bi-llah, was the ninth Umayyad Caliph of Cordova (961-976), a great patron of arts, sciences, and education, and perhaps the most scholarly ruler of Islam. He encouraged the study of mathematics, astronomy, and medicine. Owing to his interest and influence, Cordova became the second greatest city of Islam (surpassed only by Constantinople) and its university the greatest center of Islamic learning. Al Hakam sent men of learning and government officials to every part of the Moslem world to obtain manuscripts or to copy them. His library is said to have contained about 400,000 volumes, and its catalogue filled 44 volumes.

Abul Wafa, an astronomer and mathematician was one of the last Arabic translators and commentators of Greek works, dealing in particular with Euclid and Diophantus.

Hasdai ibn Shaprut was a Jewish physician and minister in al Hakam's cabinet and a translator of Greek into Arabic. He translated a manuscript of Dioscorides with the aid of a Greek monk. This manuscript had been presented to Abd al Rahman III, under whom Hasdai also served, by the Emperor Constantine VII; the Greek monk was sent to Cordova by the Emperor at the request of the Caliph to help in its translation. Hasdai was also a great patron of Jewish science and it was partly due to his influence that the intellectual center of Israel was transferred from Babylonia to Spain. The Spanish Renaissance was in the main owed to his enlightened generosity.

The first period of translation into Arabic, A.D. 650-800, represents an excellent start. To be sure, translations were few in the beginning and spaced over a long period. Thus the first hundred years of Islamic culture yielded very little, but this humble beginning furnished clues of things to come. Interest in translation was not confined to an occasional learned man; persons of high rank took an active part in this endeavor. Severus Sebokht, a churchman, and Khalid ibn Yazid ibn Murawiya, a prince and influential in government affairs, encouraged translations.

Still more important for the immense translation work to succeed, was the constant help rendered by the government and the church.

The first real harvest took place in the second half of the eighth century when translations into Arabic of Syrian, Persian, Hindu, and Greek works were being made. Again it should be emphasized here that translations into Arabic were not being done privately, occasionally, and for curiosity. Rather, there was a well-planned program backed by the government. Two of the greatest Abbasid caliphs encouraged the work of the translators who were busily unlocking the treasures of Greek knowledge. Al Mansur is given the credit for bringing to Baghdad the physician ibn Bakhtyashu, who embarked on translating into Arabic the Greek medical works, an activity which continued (with several Bakhtyashu participating) until practically all available Greek medical knowledge was translated. Al Mansur also enlisted in his service ibn al Batriq, one of the pioneer translators from Greek into Arabic, who is credited with having translated for him the major works of Galen and Hippocrates. Other protégés of Al Mansur translated Ptolemy's *Quadripartitium*, Euclid's *Elements,* and the *Almagest.* Harun al Rashid continued the search for and the translation of Greek manuscripts, mainly medical.

Thus the second half of the eighth century was a period of

transmission of knowledge and its assimilation by the Arabs. The task was not easy. George Sarton describes its problems:

> Streams of knowledge were converging in the caliphate from the Byzantine Empire, from Persia, and from India. But this new concentration was not by any means as easy as the old Alexandrian one; that had been mainly a prolongation of the Greek culture with a few foreign additions of minor importance. On the contrary, the vehicle of the new Muslim civilization was a language which had never been used before for any scientific purpose. Almost every bit of knowledge had to be translated either from Greek, from Sanskrit, or from Pahlawi, before it could be assimilated. And not only that, but these translations made necessary the creation of an entirely new philosophic and scientific terminology. Taking all this into consideration, instead of being surprised at the relative smallness of the first harvest one cannot help but admire the immensity of the effort. This effort was of such a nature that no people could have endured it for a long time, but only during a period of exaltation and youthful optimism. It must be added that the early Muslim men of science were apparently bewildered by the amount of knowledge pouring upon them from East and West and do not seem to have realized at once the overwhelming superiority of the Western sources. Indeed how could they have realized it? For at the beginning, Greek knowledge reached them only in a very impure state, after having filtered through the Byzantine and Syrian minds.[1]

As translations into Arabic increased, the march of Islam toward a leading role in culture and science also stepped up. It almost seems that translation was the driving force for Islam. It thrived as long as this activity continued.

The golden age of translation from Greek into Arabic was the ninth century. The Moslems had become the standard-bearers of civilization, largely because of the great number of works translated into Arabic. Witness the methods of transla-

---

[1] George Sarton, *Introduction to the History of Science* (Baltimore, Williams and Wilkins, 1927-1948), Vol. I, p. 523.

tions, the quantity and quality of works translated during the period, and the institutions specifically designed as centers of translation:

1. A school of translation, led by Thabit ibn Qurra, produced Arabic versions of some of the main works of the classics in the field of mathematics: Euclid, Archimedes, Apollonius, Theodosius, Ptolemy, Eutocios, and others. Thabit and his disciples, including his son and other members of his family, have been credited with translating the bulk of Greek mathematical and astronomical works.

2. The generous efforts of the three brothers Banu Musa, who, with others, paid for translations of such Greek works as the four books of Apollonius and many mathematical, mechanical, and astronomical works.

3. The great translation center Bayt al Hikma established in Baghdad by al Mamun at a cost of about a million dollars of current value, served also as a library and academy. Its first head was ibn Masawaih. Hunain ibn Ishaq, probably the greatest of all Islamic translators, succeeded ibn Masawaih, and Ishaq ibn Hunain, son of Hunain, became its third head. To the work of this translation center, Islam owed much of its vibrant energy and its flowering of science, art, and literature. Hunain ibn Ishaq concentrated on the collection of Greek medical transcripts, and together with other translators in the House of Wisdom, translated them into Arabic. His role in regard to medical literature was very similar to that of Thabit ibn Qurra in regard to mathematical and astronomical books.

4. Another school of translators, led by Qusta ibn Luqa, translated into Arabic the work of Diophantus, Theodosius, Autolycus, Hypsicles, Aristarchus, and Heron.

The ninth century had its intellectual center in Baghdad. Any translation done after 900 was anticlimatic to the work completed in the previous hundred years. It could hardly be otherwise, for by that time most of the classic Greek texts in mathematics, astronomy, and medicine had already been translated. Nevertheless, the period 900 to 1000 was not without accomplishments, nor did it lack organizational efforts to promote translations.

Among the leading patrons of science during this period were Abd al Rahman III, Caliph of Cordova; Abdu al Dawla, Sultan of Southern Persia and Iraq; and al Hakam II (ibn Abd al Rahman III). The leading Baghdad translators were Matta ibn Yunus, Yahya ibn Adi, Abu Uthman al Dimishqi, and Abul Wafa, the great Moslem mathematician. Elsewhere, the achievements of Hasdai ibn Shaprut, the Jewish physician and minister in al Hakam's cabinet, (see page XXX) marked the beginning of a movement which was to lead to Jewish intellectual ascendancy in general and to the establishment of translation centers occupied by Jewish scholars, whose importance in translating from the Arabic into Spanish and into other languages can hardly be overestimated.

SUMMARY OF ARABIC TRANSLATIONS

Most of the translators were also physicians. These medical men were the best translators. The first manuscripts to be translated were in the fields of medicine, mathematics, and astronomy —according to the Arabs, the practical arts. Translation of theoretical works did not come until later.

The knowledge translated into Arabic was from Sanskrit, Persian, Syriac, and Greek sources, the last being the most important. Most of the translators were Christians (Nestorians) and Syrians or Persians. These scholars were not only the most numerous but also the most competent. Jewish scholars participated but only later did they play a more important role in translating from Arabic into Latin.

The contributions made by Arab scholars and by Moslems of Persian origin were significant, but they consisted mainly in patronage of translation work, in establishing translation centers, and in securing Greek manuscripts.

The age of translation, lasting almost 150 years, 750-900, was followed by years of original Moslem creativity and intellectual ascendancy.

During the twelfth and thirteenth centuries, Western progress in science was so rapid that it began to overtake Moslem advances. Even at this time Islam produced great scholars in many fields of science, but their number declined.

Why did Islam falter? The causes of change were many, and some may be mentioned here.

One was the excessive growth of orthodoxy in Islam.

Furthermore, Islam ceased to make further progress in the sciences because it had reached the limit of its growth. Its greatness may have been due to intellectual precocity rather than to sustained leadership qualities; while Islam was still in its youth, it had the ingredients necessary for phenomenal growth, but the days of exaltation had come to an end.

Islam did not go beyond the achievements of Hellenistic mechanics; no new inventions of importance were made.

Islam's rise in culture and science is closely connected with translating activities; as long as these persisted, Islam was motivated to reach for greater cultural heights. But when the decline of translation work set in, Islam's cultural leadership had run its course. What Islam had set out to do—to absorb other peoples' cultures by translation—had been achieved.

CHAPTER SEVEN

The Impact of Translations on the West

Just as translations had lifted Islam to cultural leadership, so translations shocked Europe out of its long slumber and ignited the explosive development of the West. Translation on an organized basis had begun with Constantine the African (died 1087), the first great translator from Arabic into Latin, who translated many medical writings.

The real age of translation, however, did not begin until the twelfth century. At that time, and for the subsequent centuries, translation was the main intellectual task.

Here are lists, chronologically arranged, of leading translators of the various periods, together with the titles of some of the works they translated and pertinent comments. Other lists follow later in this chapter.

FIRST HALF OF THE TWELFTH CENTURY

ADELARD OF BATH — 1116-1142; *English, Christian;* Arabic into Latin

1. Astronomical tables of al Khwarizmi
2. Other mathematical treatises of al Khwarizmi
3. Euclid's fifteen books

Philosopher, mathematician, scientist, one of the most learned men before Grosseteste and Bacon and one of the earliest translators from Arabic into Latin, Adelard was instrumental in introducing some knowledge of Moslem music into the West.

JOHN OF SEVILLE — 1126-1151; *Spanish, Jewish;* Arabic into Latin

1. Al Khwarizmi's *Arithmetic*
2. Various treatises of astronomy and astrology by Mashallah (750-800)
3. *Kitab Fi Harakat al Samawiya Wa Jawami Ilm al Nujum (Elements of Astronomy)* by al Farghani
4. Abu Ali al Khaiyat's treatise on astronomy *(Ideas on the Origins of the Stars)*
5. Several of al Kindi's treatises *(On Major Conjunctions and Accurate Cycles of the Years)*
6. Abu Mashar's astronomical works *(Introduction on the Function of the Stars)*
7. Ibn al Farrukhan's astronomy *(Origin of the Stars)*
8. Commentary on Ptolemy's *Centiloquium (Astrological Treatise),* by Ahmad ibn Yusuf ibn al Daya
9. Al Battani's Astronomy *(A Treatise on Astronomy)*
10. Thabit ibn Qurra's *De imaginibus astronomicis (Astronomical Signs)*
11. Al Qabisi's *Kitab al Madkhal Ila Sinaat Ahkam al Nujum (Functions of the Planetary System)* and other works dealing with the planetary system
12. The Astrology of Maslama ibn Ahmad al Majriti
13. Part of Sir al Asrar *(Secretum Secretorum)*
14. Qusta ibn Luqa's *Kitab al Fasl bain al Ruh wal Nafs (The Difference Between Life and Death)*
15. Al Farabi's *Kitab Ihsa al Ulum (Classification and Fundamental Principles of Science)*
16. Ibn Sina's partial translation of the *Kitab al Shifa (A Philosophical Encyclopedia)*
17. Ibn Gabirol's *Yanbu al Hayat (Fountain of Life)*
18. Al Ghazzali's *Maqasid al Falasifa (Aims of Philosophers)*

Most of the translations by John of Seville were done with Domingo Gundisalvo and many of them were later again translated from Arabic into Latin. The translations cover four fields

—arithmetic, astronomy and astrology, medicine, and philosophy. The most important among these translations are al Khwarizmi's *Arithmetic*, al Farghani's *Astronomy* and the *Secret of Secrets*, and, above all, the philosophical writings of al Farabi, ibn Sina, ibn Gabirol and al Ghazzali, which were a revelation to the Latin world and deeply influenced the development of scholastic philosophy.

DOMINGO GUNDISALVO — 1126-1151; *Spanish, Christian;* Arabic into Latin

Gundisalvo was archdeacon of Segovia and worked in collaboration with John of Seville. Moslem-Jewish learning based on Greek knowledge was introduced into Latin Christendom. Gundisalvo's original writings as well as his classification of the sciences may be traced to al Farabi, ibn Sina, and others. In turn, the influence of Gundisalvo's classification of sciences can be traced to the writings of Michael Scot, Albertus Magnus, and Robert Kilwardby.

HERMAN THE DALMATIAN — 1138–1145; *Christian;* Arabic into Latin

1. Sahl ibn Bishr's astrological treatise
2. Al Khwarizmi's astronomical tables
3. Abu Mashar's *Kitab al Madkhal Ila Ilm Ahkam al Nujum (Book on Observations and Functions of the Stars)*
4. Two treatises written in Arabic against Islam
5. Ptolemy's *Planisphaerium* by Maslama ibn Ahmad al Majriti
6. Various treatises on meteorology, arithmetic, geometry, and the astrolabe

Herman studied at Chartres or Paris. Moslama ibn Ahmad al Majriti's translation of Ptolemy's *Planisphaerium* and Herman's version of it are the only ones through which the *Planisphaerium* reached the West.

HUGH OF SANTALLA — 1119-1151; *Spanish, Christian;* Arabic into Latin

1. Al Biruni's commentary on al Farghani's *Astronomy*
2. An Aristotelian treatise
3. Mashallah's meteorological predictions *De Nativitatibus* (*On Origins*) and *Liber ymbrium* (*The Book on Storms*)
4. A treatise on geomancy *Ilm al Raml* (*Science of Sand*) (as a means of fortune telling)
5. Two short treatises dealing with zoology
6. Ptolemy's *Centiloquium*
7. The earliest Latin version of the alchemical text called *The Emerald Table*

ROBERT OF CHESTER — 1141-1150; *English, Christian;* Arabic into Latin

1. Al Kindi's *Judicia* (*Judgments*)
2. First Latin translation of the *Quran*
3. Khalid ibn Yazid's alchemical treatise
4. First translation of al Khwarizmi's algebra
5. A treatise on Ptolemy's astrolabe

Archdeacon of Pamplona, English mathematician, astronomer, alchemist, Robert of Chester lived in Spain where he saw the power of Islam. The translation of the Quran was made at the request of Peter the Venerable for the purpose of refuting it.

The alchemical treatise was one of the earliest to be introduced to the Latin world. The first translation of the algebra of al Khwarizmi by Robert of Chester is dated about 1145. Its importance can hardly be overestimated. It may be said to mark the beginning of European algebra.

PLATO OF TIVOLI — 1133-1150; *Italian, Christian;* Arabic into Latin

1. Al Imrani's treatise on astrology

2. Al Khaiyat's treatise on astrology *De nativitatibus* (*On Births*)
3. Al Mansur's astrological aphorisms
4. Ptolemy's *Quadripartitum (Fourpartite)*, dealing with astrology
5. Al Farghani's *Elements of Astronomy* and some of al Battani's work on astronomy
6. Abu Bakr al Hasan ibn al Khasib's astrology *De revolutionibus nativitatum* (*On the Cycles of Births*)
7. Ibn Saffar's astrolabe *Liber Abulcasim de operibus astrolabiae (Book of Abulcasim on the Operations of the Astrolabe)*
8. Several treatises on geometry

Plato of Tivoli was aided in his translation by the Jew Abraham Bar Hiyya much in the same manner as John of Seville was assisted by Domingo Gundisalvo. In 1138 Ptolemy's *Quadripartitum* (on astrology), was translated from the Arabic. This was the first of Ptolemy's works to be translated into Latin. We should note here that Abraham Bar Hiyya translated from the Hebrew (he was one of the few at that time to translate from the Hebrew into Latin) a treatise on practical geometry. This translation is of fundamental importance as it was one of the main sources for Fibonacci, the mathematician.

STEPHEN OF ANTIOCH — *c.* 1128, *perhaps of Italian extraction, Christian;* Arabic into Latin

Kitab al Maliki of Ali ibn Abbas.

Stephen was born in Pisa, educated in Salerno, and lived in Antioch.

JAMES OF VENICE — 1128-1136: *Italian, Christian;* Greek into Latin

In about 1128 he translated the *Topics,* the *Prior* and *Posterior Analytics* and the *Sophistici elenchi* (*Sophistical Index*). These parts of the Aristotelian *Organon* which he was the first, after Boetius, to reveal to the Latin West were called the "New Logic." This New Logic reached the West a little later, through another channel, the translation from the Arabic by Gerard of Cremona (1114-1187).

ABRAHAM IBN EZRA — 1140-1146; *Spanish, Jew;* Arabic into Hebrew

1. Three treatises on grammar
2. Two treatises on astrology by Mashallah
3. Al Biruni's commentary on al Khwarizmi's tables

Abraham ibn Ezra traveled extensively in France and England. He was the first to translate Moslem writings into Hebrew. He helped to propagate among the Jews of Christian Europe the rationalistic attitudes that had been developed in Spain by Moslems and Jews on the basis of Greco-Moslem knowledge and was much admired by Spinoza on that account.

ABRAHAM BAR HIYYA — 1133-1150; *Spanish, Jew;* Arabic into Latin and Hebrew

1. With Plato of Tivoli and Rudolph of Bruges, scientific works into Latin.
2. A musical treatise, Arabic into Hebrew; a leader of the movement which caused the Jews of Provence, Spain, and Italy to become the transmitters of Moslem science to the Christian West. Abraham also may have been one of the links through which Moslem music reached the West. His influential treatise on geometry was translated into Latin in 1145.

Much of the knowledge available in Europe during the period 1100-1150 was obtained by translations from foreign languages, chiefly Arabic. The center of translation for most of the period was in Spain, mostly in Toledo. There were three reasons for this. Toledo had been in Moslem hands from 712 to 1085. Though it was reconquered, it offered an abundance of Arabic writings. Even more important, a large part of Toledo's population—Jews, Moslems, Christians—used Arabic as their own language. In addition, Archbishop Raymond I (1126-1151) organized a school of translators which, in cooperation with dragomans (interpreters), made excellent translations. Native assistance is essential to make sure that idiomatic meanings are not misunderstood. Translators usually worked in pairs, like John of Seville and Domingo Gundisalvo.

There were also translations from Arabic into languages other than Latin. Translations from Arabic into Hebrew were still insignificant, and the number of Jews engaged in the art of transmitting knowledge from the Arabic were few. This is easily explained by the fact that Eastern and most Spanish Jewish scholars were not only sufficiently well conversant with Arabic not to need such translations, but often had a better knowledge of Arabic than of Hebrew. Nonetheless, the translations that were made did as much to further the education of European Jews as the translations into Latin did to enlighten European Christians. Thus, Moslem science and culture penetrated western Europe through more than one channel.

There were also other translations—Latin into French, Celtic into Latin, Hebrew into Latin, and Greek into Latin. The last was by far the most important. These translations spread rapidly among the learned men of Europe. The following conclusions may be drawn with respect to this period.

1. Greek science and culture were being introduced into the West through three channels: a direct one, Greek into Latin; and indirect ones, Arabic into Latin, and Arabic into Hebrew. The most important was the Arabic into Latin.

2. The main work of translation was done in Spain by Christians with the help of Jews.

3. Churchmen took a most active part in the transmitting of knowledge, either directly or as patrons of translators.

4. The awakening of Europe, begun in the last half of the eleventh century, was sparked by the translations of Constantine the African in the field of medicine. The ensuing activities in the twelfth century were immense, almost as lively as in the eighth and ninth centuries of Islam. Countries sharing in the revival included Italy, Germany, England, and Spain. The re-awakening of Europe was decisively helped by translations, and translations served as a continuum in the revival of Europe.

SECOND HALF OF THE TWELFTH CENTURY

GERARD OF CREMONA — 1114-1187; *Italian, Christian;* Arabic into Latin

Logic:

1. Aristotle, *Posterior Analytics,* two books from the Arabic version by Matta ibn Yunus (first half of tenth century)
2. Themistios (late fourth century), *Commentary on the Posterior Analytics,* one book, probably from the same Arabic version
3. Al Farabi, *De syllogismo (On the Syllogism),* a part of his elaboration on Aristotle's *Organon*

Philosophy: Nos. 4 to 10 are Aristotelian or pseudo-Aristotelian writings; Nos. 11 to 15 are Aristotelian commentaries by Alexander of Aphrodisias

4. *De coelo et mundo (On Heaven and the Earth),* four books
5. *De naturali auditu (On Natural Hearing),* eight books
6. *De generatione et corruptione (On Generation and Corruption)*
7. *Liber meteororum (Book of Meteors),* Books I to IV, from the Arabic version by Yahya ibn Batriq; Book IV had been translated before
8. *Liber lapidum (Book of Gems),* a work quoted by the German author of an encyclopedia, Arnold of Saxony (early thirteenth century)

9. *De expositione bonitatis purae (On the Exposition of Pure Goodness)* and the famous Neoplatonic *Liber de causis (Book of Diseases)*

10. *De elementis* or *De proprietatibus elementorum (On the Elements or On the Properties of Elements),* in all probability a Moslem work

11. *De motu et tempore (On Motion and Time)*

12. *De sensu (On Perception)*

13. *De eo quod augmentum et incrementum fiunt in forma et non in yle (On the Idea that Growth and Increase Take Place in Form and not in Matter)* from the Arabic version of Abu Uthman Sa'id al Dimishqi (early tenth century)

14. *De intellectu et intellecto (On the Intellect and the Thing Understood),* from the Arabic version of Hunain ibn Ishaq, printed 1501

15. *De unitate*

16. Al Kindi, *De quinque essentiis (sive substantiis) (On the Five Essences or Substances)*

17. Al Kindi, *De somno et visione (On Sleep and Dreaming)*

18. Al Kindi, *De ratione* (or *Verbum de intentione antiquorum in ratione) (On Reason)*

19. Al Farabi, *Distinctio super librum Aristotelis de naturali auditu (Criticism of the Book of Aristotle on Natural Hearing)*

20. Al Farabi, *De scientiis (On Sciences).* There is an earlier translation or adaptation by Gundisalvo. Gerard's version was published by Guilelmus Camerarius (Paris 1638); Gundisalvo's by Clemens Baeumker (Münster 1916; Isis, 4 135). A Hebrew version was edited by Mich. Rosenstein (Breslau 1858).

21. Ishaq al Israili, *De elementis (On the Elements),* printed in the *Omnia Opera Isaac (Complete Works of Isaac)* (Lyon 1515). This text had not been translated by Constantine the African.

22. Ishaq al Israili, *De descriptione rerum et definitionibus earum et de differentia inter descriptionem et definitionem (On the Description of Things, Their Definitions and the Difference Between Description and Definition)*.

Greek mathematics and astronomy:

23. Autolycus, *De sphaera mota (On the Sphere in Motion)* from the Arabic version by Ishaq ibn Hunain and Qusta ibn Luqa

24. Euclid, *Elements*, fifteen books (long believed lost, but A. A. Björnbo discovered various manuscripts in 1904 which he identified as Gerard's version)

25. Euclid, *Data*, from the Arabic version by Ishaq ibn Hunain, revised by Thabit ibn Qurra

26. Archimedes, *De mensura circuli (On Measuring the Circle)*

27. Apollonius, *Conics*. The ascription of the Latin version to Gerard of Cremona was made by Heiberg.

28. Hypsicles (early second century B.C.), from the Arabic version by Ishaq ibn Hunain and Qusta ibn Luqa

29. Theodosius (early first century B.C.), *De sphaeris*

30. Theodosius, *De locis habitabilibus (On Habitable Places)* from the Arabic version by Qusta ibn Luqa

31. Geminos (early first century B.C.), *Liber introductorius ad artem sphaericam (Introduction to the Use of the Sphere)*

32. Menelaos (late first century), *De figuris sphaericis (On Spherical Figures)*

33. Ptolemy, *Liber almagesti*, completed by Gerard at Toledo in 1175 and printed in Venice in 1515

Arabic mathematics and astronomy:

34. Banu Musa, *Liber trium fratrum (Book of Three Brothers)*, edited by Max Curtze (Halle 1885)

35. Al Khwarizmi, *De algebra et almucabala*, edited by Guillaume Libri under the title *Histoire des sciences mathématiques*

36. Al Farghani, *De aggregationibus scientiae stellarum et de principiis coelestium motuum (On the Collections of Knowledge of the Stars and the Principles of Heavenly Movements)*. An earlier translation by John of Seville was printed in Ferrara in 1493. The Latin text (probably Gerard's) was translated into French and from French into Italian by Zucchero Bencivenni in 1313. Gerard's translation was paraphrased in Hebrew by Jacob Anatoli about 1232; and Anatoli's Hebrew version was retranslated into Latin by Jacob Christmann (Frankfort 1590).

37. Ahmad ibn Yusuf, *De arcubus similibus, (On Similar Arcs)* edited by Max. Curtze (Mitt. des Copernikus Vereins, 48-50, 1887)

38. Ahmad ibn Yusuf, *De proportione et proportionalitate (On Proportion and the Relation of Proportion)*

39. Al Nairizi, *Commentary on Euclid's Elements, Books I to X*, edited by M. Curtze, as supplement to Heiberg and Menge's edition of Euclid (420 p., Leipzig 1899)

40. Thabit ibn Qurra, *De figura alchata*

41. Thabit ibn Qurra, *De expositione nominum Almagesti (Explication of the Names of the Almagest)*

42. Thabit ibn Qurra, *De motu accessionis et recessionis (On Forward and Backward Motion)*, printed under the title *De motu octavae sphaerae (The Motion of the Eighth Sphere)* (1480, 1509, 1518)

43. Abu *Kamil, Liber qui secundum Arabes vocatur algebra et almucabala (The Book Called by the Arabs Algebra and Almucabala)*

44. Abu Uthman, or Muhammad ibn 'Abd al Baqi, *Liber Judaei super decimum Euclidis (Book of the Jew on Euclid's Tenth)*, edited under the title *De numeris et lineis (On Numbers and Lines)* by B. Boncompagni 1863 and by M. Curtze (Leipzig 1899)

45. 'Arib ibn Sa'd, a work on a Christian calendar containing astronomical and agricultural information, edited by G. Libri, in his *Histoire des sciences mathematiques*
46. Jabir ibn Aflah, *Gebri De astronomia libri IX in quibus Ptolemaeum emendavit* (*The Nine Books on Astronomy in which Ptolemy is Corrected*) (Nuremberg 1534)
47. *De practica geometriae* (*On Practical Geometry*), of unknown date and authorship
48. *Algorismus in integris et minutiis* (*Algorismus on Whole Numbers and Fractions*), an unidentified arithmetic; the translator is called Gernandus
49. *Liber coaequationis planetarum* (*Book on the Equilibrium of the Planets*)

The two following items are astronomical tables:
50. Al Zarqali, *Canones Arzachelis*. There are many manuscripts of the Latin version of these very popular tables, but some of them which do not bear Gerard's name may represent other versions.
51. *Liber omnium sphaerarum coeli et compositionis tabularum* (*Book of All the Heavenly Spheres and The Arrangement of Tables*)

Physics and Mechanics:
52. Diocles, *De speculis comburentibus* (*On Burning Mirrors*); *Liber Tidei de speculo* (*The Book of Tideus on the Mirror*), as transmitted by a commentary of Eutocios on Archimedes
53. Al Kindi, *De aspectibus* (*On Appearances*), followed by *De umbris et de diversitate aspectuum* (*On Shadows and the Diversity of Appearances*), edited by A. A. Björnbo and Seb. Vogl (Leipzig 1912)
54. Thabit ibn Qurra, *Liber charastonis* (*Qurra's Book*) (F. Buchner: Die Schrift über den Qarastun; Sitzungsber. der phys. med. Soz., vol. 52, 141-188, Erlangen 1922; Isis, 5 494).

55. Ibn al Haitham, *De crepusculis et nubium ascensionibus (On Twilight and the Gathering of Clouds)*, printed in Lisbon in 1542 and in Basle in 1572.

Greek Medicine:

56. *Liber veritatis Hippocratis de istis qui laborant in agone mortis (The Book of Truth of Hippocrates on Those in the Throes of Death)*, also called *Liber sapientiae et Capsula eburnea (Book of Wisdom and Ivory Box)*. There are various Arabic versions of this pseudo-Hippocratic treatise, one by Yahya ibn Batriq, another by Hunain ibn Ishaq, printed together with Razi's *Liber ad Almansorem* (1497, 1500).

57. Commentary on Hippocrates' *Regimen acutarum aegritudinum (The Regimen of Dangerous Illnesses)*

The following items (58 to 66) of this section are Galenic or pseudo-Galenic writings, all of which were probably translated into Arabic by Hunain; No. 64 may have been translated by Yahya ibn Batriq.

58. Commentary on Hippocrates' *Prognostica (Prognostics)*, same text previously translated by Constantine the African

59. *De elementis (On the Elements)*

60. *De secretis ad Monteum (On Secrets to Monteus)*

61. *De complexionibus (On Complications)*

62. *De malicia complexionis diversa (On the Evil of Varied Complication)*

63. *De simplici medicina (On Simple Medicine)*, or *De simplicibus medicamentis (On Simple Remedies)*

64. *De criticis diebus (On the Days of Crisis)*

65. *De crisi (On Crises)*

Arabic Medicine:

66. Al Kindi, *De gradibus medicinarum (On the Range of Medicines)* or *De medicinarum compositarum gradibus investigandis (On Investigating the Range of Compound*

Medicines), printed with the Latin translation of ibn Butlan's Tacuinum (Strasbourg 1531); also in *Opusculum
de dosibus* (Brief Work on Doses) (Venice 1556); the
same text was also translated by Arnold of Villanova.

67. Ibn Masawaih, *Aphorisms*

68. Yahya ibn Sarafyun, *Breviarium (Breviary); Practica Joan-
nis Serapionis dicta breviarium (The Practice of John Sera-
pion Called the Breviary)* (Venice 1497)

69. Al Razi, *Liber Albubatri Rasis qui dicitur Almansorius
(Book of Albutrus Rasis Known as Almansor)*

70. Al Razi, *Liber divisionum continens CLIIII capitula cum
quibusdam confectionibus ejusdem (Book of Divisions
Containing 154 Chapters with Certain Prescriptions of the
Same Author)*

71. Al Razi, *Liber introductorius in medicinam parvus (Brief
Introduction to Medicine)*

72. Al Razi, *De juncturarum aegritudinibus (On Sicknesses of
the Joints)*, Nos. 70 to 73 are included in Razi's *Opera*
(Venice 1500), together with a few other texts.

73. Abu-l-Qasim, *Liber Azaragui de chirurgia (Book of Azara-
guus on Surgery)*, first printed together with Chauliac's
Latin surgery (Venice 1498, etc.)

74. Ibn Sina, *Canon Avicennae libri quinque (Five Books of
the Canon of Avicenna)*, often printed: Milan 1473, Padua
1476, (at least fifteen incunabula editions)

75. Ibn al Wafid, *De medicinis et cibis simplicibus (On Medicines and Simple Foods)*, or *De simplicium medicinarum
virtutibus (On the Powers of Simple Medicines)*, printed
with ibn Butlan's *Tacuinum* (Strasbourg, 1531)

76. 'Ali ibn Ridwan, commentary on Galen's *Tegni* (Ars Medica), the so-called *Microtegni*

Arabic astrology:

77. *Liber alfadhol, id est arab de bachi (Book of Alfadhol, that
is, The Arab of Bachus)*, possibly by al Fadl ibn Naubakht

(late eighth century) or al Fadl ibn Sahl al Sarakhsi (early
ninth century)

78. Mashallah, *De orbe,* also *De scientia motus orbis (On the
Science of the Movement of the World); De elementis et
orbibus coelestibus (On Elements and Heavenly Orbs);
De ratione circuli coelestis (On the Nature of the Heavenly
Circle); De natura orbium (On the Nature of Orbs),* printed
in Nuremberg in 1504 and 1549

79. "Alchandrus," "Alcandrinus" (late tenth century), *Arcan-
dam de veritatibus et praedictionibus astrologiae (Ar-
candam on the Truths and Predictions of Astrology)* (Paris
1542)

80. *Liber in quo terrarum corporumque continentur mensur-
ationes Abhabuchri, qui dicebatur Heus (Book Containing
the Measurements of Lands and Bodies of Abhabuchri,
Called Heus),* author unidentified

81. *Liber de accidentibus alfel (Book of Ominous Events).*
Alfel is a corruption of an Arabic word which is taken as
an omen.

82. Jabir ibn Haiyan, *Liber divinitatis de LXX (Book of Di-
vinity of the 70)*

83. Al Razi, *De aluminibus et salibus (On Alums and Salts).*
The ascription to al Razi occurs in one manuscript, but
another contains the phrase, "apud nos in Yspania," (with
us in Spain).

84. *Liber luminis luminum (Book of the Light of Lights);
Liber qui dicitur lumen luminum et perfecti magisterii
(Book Called Light of Lights and Perfect Instruction),* also
ascribed to al Razi, but according to F. Wustenfeld (no.
67, 1877) this does not seem to be a translation from the
Arabic.

85. *Liber geomantiae de artibus divinatoriis (Book of Geomancy
on the Arts of Divination)*

Gerard of Cremona was perhaps the greatest of all translators.
He was anxious to translate the *Almagest,* which was not then

available in Latin. He therefore journeyed to Toledo where he studied Arabic and worked as a translator until his death. Seventy-one works were purportedly translated by him, which he could not possibly have done unassisted, but he may have been the head of a school of translation.

MARC OF TOLEDO — 1190-1200; Spanish, Christian; Arabic into Latin

1. The Quran
2. Galenic treatises from the Arabic version of Hunain ibn Ishaq
3. Several other treatises of Hunain ibn Ishaq's works

JOSEPH QIMHI — c. 1150; Spanish, Jewish; Arabic into Hebrew

1. *Kitab al Hidayat Ila Faraid al Qulub* of Bahya Ben Joseph (*Ethics*)
2. He continued the activity of Abraham ibn Ezra and Abraham Bar Hiyya as translator of Judeo-Arabic thought to the Jews of Christian Europe.

JUDAH IBN TIBBON — 1150-1180; Spanish, Jewish; Arabic into Latin

1. Saadia Ben Joseph's *Kitab al Amanat Walitiqadat* (*Faiths and Dogmas*)
2. Ibn Gabirol's *Kitab Islah al Akhlaq* (*Correction of Manners*)
3. Ibn Jonah's *Kitab al Luma* (*Grammar*) and *Kitab al Usul* (*Dictionary* or *Book of Origins*)
4. Judah ha Levi's *Kitab al Hujjah* (*Pilgrimage*)
5. Bahya Ben Joseph's *Kitab al Hidayat Ila Faraid al Qulub*

Judah ibn Tibbon has been called the "father of Jewish translators"; he recommended that his son read as much Arabic as possible to keep in good order the large Hebrew and Arabic library he was bequeathing to him and to translate as much as possible. Samuel ibn Tibbon, the son to whom this advice was directed, became a great translator in the early thirteenth century.

EUGENE THE AMIR — 1150-1160; Greek, Christian; Arabic and Greek into Latin

1. *The Optics,* ascribed to Ptolemy, from Arabic
2. *Almagest,* from Greek

Eugene the Amir flourished under Roger II and William I, Kings of Sicily, and was a member of the administration of William I; he was a mathematician, astronomer, and also helped to transmit to the West the fables of Kalila Wa Dimna.

ARISTIPPUS OF CATANIA — *c.* 1160; Sicilian, Christian; Greek into Latin

1. *The Meno* and *Phaedo* of Plato
2. The fourth book of Aristotle's *Meteorology*

An archdeacon of Catania, on the east coast of Sicily, Aristippus brought Greek manuscripts from the library of Manuel I Comnenos to Sicily. His were the first translations of Plato's *Meno* and *Phaedo.*

PASCHAL THE ROMAN — 1158-1166; Italian, Christian; Greek into Latin

1. Dialogue between a Jew and a Christian
2. Compiled from Latin, Greek, and Oriental sources *Liber thesauri occulti (Book of Secret Treasure)*
3. *Cyranides,* a compendium of ancient lore on the virtues of animals, stones, and plants

WILLIAM LE MIRE — *c.* 1168; French, Christian; Greek into Latin

1. Summaries of the letters of St. Paul, and other works.

William Le Mire was abbot of St. Denis, Paris; he was sent to Constantinople to bring manuscripts to St. Denis to translate

JOHN SARAZIN — *c.* 1160; Greek into Latin

He visited the Near East in search of Greek manuscripts and translated some of the works of pseudo-Dionysios.

BURGUNDIO OF PISA — 1150-1158; Italian, Christian; Greek into Latin

1. Hippocrates, *Aphorisms*
2. Galen, *De sectis medicorum (On Classes of Physicians); De temperamentis (On Temperaments); De virtutibus (On Skills); De sanitate tuenda (On Preserving Health); De differentiis febrium (On the Differences of Fevers); De locis affectis (On Diseased Spots); De compendiositate pulsus (On Rapid Pulses); De crisibus (On Crises); Therapeutica (Therapeutics); De differentiis pulsuum (On Differences of Pulses)*
3. *De natura hominis (On the Nature of Man)*
4. Various homilies by St. John Chrysostom and St. Basil
5. John of Damascus, *De orthodoxa fide* (the main part of the *Fountain of Knowledge*)
6. Greek quotations in the *Digest* (of Greek works)

LEO TUSCUS or *Leo the Pisan* — *c.* 1176; Greek into Latin

He translated the dreambook of Ahmad Ibn Sirin from a Greek version. Leo was a member of the Pisa colony of Constantinople.

BERAKYA BEN NATRONAI HA-NAQDAN; French-Jewish moralist and translator

The twelfth century was a period in which translation from Arabic into Latin dominated all other achievements. In addition, this period was graced by perhaps the greatest translator of all times, Gerard of Cremona, who transmitted a large bulk of alien culture to his own. Gerard has been seen as an exponent of contemporary Christendom symbolic of its eagerness to learn from

Arabic sources. The impact of his translations was enormous. The Latin revival symbolized by Gerard of Cremona was essentially a revival of the natural sciences, not of the humanities, which was to come only in the Renaissance of the fifteenth century. Since Gerard spent most of his time in Toledo, Spain continued to be the world center of culture. Gerard's unparalleled activity in the field of translation generously opened to the Latin world the treasures of Greek and Arabic philosophy, mathematics, astronomy, physics, medicine, and alchemy. Of the seventy-one works which he translated, perhaps the *Almagest* and the *Qanun* of ibn Sina are the two most important. Arabic knowledge was also transmitted by means of Hebrew versions of Arabic writing. Judah ibn Tibbon and Joseph Qimhi thus continued the tradition of Abraham ibn Ezra and Abraham Bar Hiyya.

Important also were the direct translations from Greek into Latin, often inspired by previous translations from Arabic versions of Greek works.

The transmission of Arabic knowledge to the West helped to pave the way for the founding of universities. By the end of the twelfth century the universities of Salerno and Bologna had been founded in Italy, those of Paris and Montpellier in France, and of Oxford in England. An offshoot of Paris established Cambridge in 1209. A systematic method of higher education had become both possible and necessary.

FIRST HALF OF THE THIRTEENTH CENTURY

ALFRED OF SARESHEL — c. 1200; English, Christian; Arabic into Latin

1. Aristotelian treatise *De Plantis* (*On Plants*) translated into Arabic by Ishaq ibn Hunain
2. Alchemical section of ibn Sina's *Shifa*, usually referred to as *Mineralia* (*Minerals*)

Alfred of Sareshel lived and worked in Spain. His commentary on meteorology was used by Roger Bacon; his knowledge of Aristotle was unusual for his time.

MICHAEL SCOT — *c.* 1200-1235; Scotch, Christian; Arabic into Latin

1. Al Bitruji's *Kitab al Haia (Spiral Motions of the Heavenly Bodies)* was translated into Hebrew and later into Latin. Scot's version introduced al Bitruji's astronomy and the theory of the impetus into the Latin world.
2. Aristotle's *De coelo et mundo (On Heaven and the World)* with ibn Rushd's commentary
3. First Latin translation of Aristotle's *Historia animalium, (History of Animals)* nineteen books, including *De animalibus historia (History of Animals); De partibus animalium (On the Parts of Animals); De generatione animalium (On the Generation of Animals).* The translation remained in use until the fifteenth century.
4. Aristotle's *De anima (On the Soul)*, with ibn Rushd's commentary; also *De generatione et corruptione (On Generation and Corruption); Meteora (Meteors)* (Book IV of the middle commentary); *Parva naturalia (Small Objects in Nature); De substantia orbis (On the Substance of the World); Physics, Metaphysics,* and *Ethics*
5. *Divisio philosophica,* dealing with the classification of science, based on al Farabi's work (as adapted by Gundisalvo)
6. An Averroistic compendium
7. *Abbreviatio Avicennae de animalibus (Abridgment of Avicenna on Animals)*
8. Three popular treatises on astrology
9. *Liber introductorius (Introductory Book* or *Introduction)* an introduction to astrology
10. Popular introduction to astrology

11. *Physiognomia* (*Physiognomy*) the most popular of his works, includes the treatise *De urinis* (*On Urines*)
12. Treatise on alchemy, which affords evidence of collaboration with Jewish and Moslem experimenters
13. Maimonides' *Guide for the Perplexed*
14. Maimonides' *Kitab al Faraid* (*Book on the Divine Precepts*)
15. Commentary on Sacrobosco's *Sphaera*
16. *Liber geomantiae* (*Book of Geomancy*)
17. *Mensa philosophica* (*The Philosopher's Banquet*)

Scot was one of the founders of Latin Averroism, the school of thought of Averroës (ibn Rushd). His main achievements, however, were his translations, not only of ibn Rushd, but also of Aristotle and al Bitruji from the Arabic into Latin. Scot was for many years in the service of Frederick II as a professional translator and an experimental philosopher. He became famous as an astrologer, alchemist and magician. Dante put him in Hell (XX 116).

STEVEN OF SARAGOSSA — *c.* 1230; Spanish, Christian; Arabic into Latin
1. Al Jazzar's *Kitab Itimad Fil Adwiya al Mufrada* (*Treatise on Reliable and Simple Drugs*)

PETER GALLEGO — *c.* 1230; Spanish, Christian; Arabic into Latin
1. Aristotle's treatise on animals from an Arabic abridgment
2. A treatise on economy, probably that of pseudo-Galen

SALIO OF PADUA — *c.* 1240; Spanish, Christian; Arabic into Latin
1. Abu Bakr's astrological treatise

WILLIAM OF LUNIS — *c.* 1230; Italian, Christian; Arabic into Latin
1. Ibn Rushd's commentaries on Aristotelian logic.

PHILIP OF TRIPOLI — *c.* 1233; Syrian, Christian; Arabic into Latin
1. Sir al Asrar (the pseudo-Aristotelian *Secret of Secrets*)

IBN HASDAI — 1225-1240; Spanish, Jew; Arabic into Hebrew

1. *Kitab al Tuffahah (Book of the Apple)*
2. *Kitab al Istaqisat by Ishaq al Israili (Treatise on the Elements)*
3. *Mizan al Amal*, an ethical treatise by al Ghazzali
4. Two treatises by Maimonides *(Lists of Prohibitive and Mandatory Commandments)*
5. The story of Barlaam and Ioasaph (A famous religious romance of the Middle Ages)

SAMUEL IBN TIBBON — *c.* 1200; Spanish, Jew; Arabic into Hebrew

1. Yahya ibn Batriq's Arabic version of Aristotle's *Meteorology*
2. Ali ibn Ridwan's commentary on Galen's *Tegni (Ars Medica)* the so-called *Microtegni*
3. Ibn Rushd's three small treatises, translated under the title *Sheloshah Maamarim Philosophical Commentaries*
4. Maimonides, *Dalalat al Hairin (Guide for the Perplexed)*
5. Maimonides' treatise on resurrection
6. Maimonides' Mishna *Ethics* taken from *Kitab al Siraj* commentary on *Pirqe abot*
7. Maimonides, *Thirteen Articles*
8. Maimonides' letter to his disciple Joseph Ibn Aqnin
9. Several Biblical commentaries

Samuel ibn Tibbon was the son of the Andalusian scholar Judah ibn Tibbon; he worked mainly in Alexandria and Marseilles. Samuel ibn Tibbon was a theologian and philosopher. The diffusion of Maimonides' philosophy in the West was largely due to his efforts.

JACOB ANATOLI — *c.* 1230-1250; French, Jew; Arabic and Latin into Hebrew

1. Ibn Rushd's intermediate commentaries on Porphyry's *Isagoge* and on Aristotle's *Categories, Interpretation, Prior* and *Posterior Analytics*

2. Ptolemy's *Almagest* from the Arabic
3. Ibn Rushd's summary of the *Almagest*
4. Al Farghani's *Kitab Fi Harkat al Samawiya*
5. Al Farabi's logical treatise

Jacob Anatoli was born in France, and was in the service of Frederick II. He was a disciple and son-in-law of Samuel ibn Tibbon. He was the first translator of ibn Rushd's commentaries into Hebrew and one of the first popularizers of Maimonides' philosophy.

AL BUNDARI — *c.* 1230; Moslem, Persian into Arabic

1. Firdawsi's *Shahanama* into Arabic for al Muazzam, ruler of Damascus (1218-1227)

JOHN OF BASINGSTOKE — *c.* 1240; English, Christian; Greek into Latin

1. Greek grammar

ROBERT GROSSETESTE — *c.* 1240; English, Christian; Greek into Latin

1. First complete translation of *Nicomachean Ethics*
2. Various other works of Aristotle and John of Damascus

Grosseteste was the first chancellor of the University of Oxford and a teacher of St. Thomas and Roger Bacon. He also exerted great influence on Albertus Magnus.

By the beginning of the thirteenth century, many of the main works were already translated. While this period produced no one comparable to Gerard, distinguished scholars devoted all or a large part of their lives to translating Arabic treatises into Latin. Translations were made at this time from Arabic into Latin, Arabic into Hebrew, Persian into Arabic, and Greek into Latin. The Arabic into Latin were by far the most important.

English and Scottish, Spanish, Italian, Syrian, and French translators transmitted Arabic knowledge into Latin. Each group contributed only one or two translators, the most remarkable men being the Englishman Alfred of Sareshel and the Scot, Michael Scot. Alfred's own treatise *De Motu Cordis (On the Motion of the Heart)* was derived largely from Arabic sources. Scot's contributions were even more important. By his translations from Arabic into Latin, he introduced three novelties of great consequence—Aristotelian zoology, Alpetragian (al Bitruji) astronomy, and ibn Rushd's philosophy. Ibn Rushd wrote in the twelfth century. Thus the Latin world knew of a Moslem achievement while it was fresh and alive. This was the first time that the most important texts to be translated were the latest. The efforts of Michael Scot, who was also one of the leading philosophers of this period, the awakening of Latindom, and the increasing drowsiness of Islam, all combined to make it possible for ibn Rushd's philosophy to reach and influence the West at a time when the majority of Moslems were still unaware of it. Moreover, the Englishman and the Scot represented a new type of translator in that they spent only part of their activity on translations; they spent more time on original research and were freer in their translations. Both were trained in Spain, and Scot did his best translations in Toledo. The Spanish schools of translators were never more international than at this time. Many foreigners were attracted to Spain as the foremost center of Arabic research.

The golden age of translation from Arabic into Hebrew began with the advent of the thirteenth century. Earlier Jewish translators had been primarily interested in Jewish works. Two of the greatest translators of medieval times came to the fore, Samuel ibn Tibbon and Jacob Anatoli. Ibn Tibbon made available to the Hebrew-speaking world Maimonides' *Guide for the Perplexed;* his son-in-law Anatoli made the first translations of ibn Rushd's commentaries. Thus Anatoli rendered to the Jews the same service that Scot rendered to the Christians.

SECOND HALF OF THE THIRTEENTH CENTURY

ARNOLD OF VILLANOVA — *c.* 1260, Christian, Italian: Arabic into Latin

1. Galen, *De tremore, palpitatione, rigore et convulsione (On Trembling, Palpitation, Stiffness and Convulsion)*, from the Arabic version by Hubaish ibn al Hasan
2. Al Kindi, *Risala Fi-marifat quwa-L-Adwiya al Murakkaba (Principles of Medicine)*
3. Qusta ibn Luqa, *(The Magical Treatise)*
4. Ibn Sina, *De viribus cordis (On the Powers of the Heart)*
5. Abu-L-Ala Zuhr, *De conservatione corporis et regimine sanitatis (On the Conservation of the Body and the Regimen of Health)*
6. Abu-L-Salt Umaiya ibn Abd al Aziz, *Kitab al Adwiya al Mufrada (The Simple Medicine)*

GIOVANNI CAMPANUS — *c.* 1260; Christian, Italian; Arabic into Latin

1. Euclid's *Elements,* Books I to XV, based upon the translations from Adelard of Bath. Campanus availed himself also of other Arabic sources. Campanus was chaplain to Urban IV, pope from 1261 to 1264. He was influenced by Grosseteste and praised by Roger Bacon.

ROBERT THE ENGLISHMAN — *c.* 1270; Christian, Englishman; Arabic into Latin. He lived and worked in Paris; his writings were derived in part from such Arabic sources as ibn Rushd and Thabit ibn Qurra.

WILLIAM OF MOERBEKE — 1260-1281; Flemish, Christian; Greek into Latin

1. Hippocrates, *Prognostics*
2. Aristotle, *Rhetoric, Politics, History of Generation of Animals,* fourth book of *Meteorology, Economics,* eleventh

book of *Metaphysics,* other books of the *Meteorology* and *Metaphysics* and the *De anima (On the Soul)*
3. Archimedes, *De iis quae in humido vehuntur (On the Things Borne About by Moisture)*
4. Hero, *Catoptrics*
5. Galen, *De Alimentis (On Foods)*
6. Alexander of Aphrodisias, commentaries on the *Meteorology* and on the *De Sensu et Sensibili (On Sensation and Things Sensible)*
7. Themistios, commentary on the *Prior Analytics* and the *De anima (On the Soul)*
8. Proclos, theological introduction
9. Proclos, commentary on the *Timaeos* and *Parmenides*
10. Philoponos, commentary on the third book of the *De anima (On the Soul)*
11. Simplicios, commentaries on the *De coelo et mundo (On Heaven and the World)* and on the *Categories*

William was chaplain to many popes, and archbishop of Corinth. Many of his translations were done at the request of St. Thomas Aquinas, including Aristotle's *Politics,* which had been hitherto unknown to the Western Christians as well as to the Moslems. Its dissemination marked the beginning of a new development of social philosophy in the Christian West.

BARTHOLOMEW OF MESSINA — 1258-1266; Messina, Naples, Sicily, Christian; Greek into Latin

1. Aristotle's *Magna moralia (The Great Books of Morals);* the *Problems* and other pseudo-Aristotelian treatises; *De principiis (On Principles); De mirabilibus auscultationibus (On Remarkable Hearings); Physiognomia (Physiognomy); De signis (On Signs)*
2. Hierocles' treatise on the veterinary art

He worked at the court of Manfred, King of Naples and Sicily.

BONACOSA — *c.* 1255; probably a Jew, translated

Ibn Rushd's *Kulliyat Fil Tibb (Medical Encyclopedia)* from Arabic (or from Hebrew) into Latin

JOHN OF BRESCIA — *c.* 1263; Italian, Christian; Arabic into Latin

He translated with Jacob Ben Mahir at Montpellier Al Zarquali's treatise on the astrolabe, *Liber tabulae quae nominatur sophaea patris Isaac Arzachelis (Book of the Table Called Wisdom of Father Isaac Arzachelis)*. Jacob translated from Arabic into the vernacular, and John wrote the Latin equivalent.

ARMENGUAD, SON OF BLAISE — *c.* 1290; French, Christian; Arabic into Latin

1. Galen's ethical treatise previously translated into Arabic by Tuma al Ruhawi, *Kitab Kaifa Yata Araf al Insan Dhunubhi Wa Uyubhi (How Man Recognizes His Sins and Vices)*
2. Pseudo-Galen, *Economy*
3. Ibn Sina, *Al Arjuzat Fil Tibb*, (A Medical Poem) together with ibn Rushd's commentary
4. Maimonides, *Maqala Fi Tadbir al Sihha (Steps to Good Health)*
5. Maimonides, *Al Sumum Wal Mutaharriz (Poisons and Antidotes)*
6. Jacob Ben Mahir, Treatise on the quadrant translated from the Hebrew

Armenguard was a physician to the king of Aragon and to Pope Clement V as well as a translator. The *Economy* referred to above deals with household management and includes morality and hygiene as well as domestic economy. This text is a Latin abridgment of the Arabic version of a Greek treatise.

HERMAN THE GERMAN — Christian; Arabic into Latin

1. Ibn Rushd, middle commentary on Aristotle's *Ethics*
2. Ibn Rushd, middle commentary on Aristotle's *Rhetoric* and *Poetic*
3. Al Farabi, commentary on the *Rhetoric*
4. *Summa quorundam Alexandrinorum (Summa of certain Alexandrines)*, relative to *Ethics*

Herman was in the service of Manfred, King of Naples, but worked in Toledo. He is said to have been the teacher of Bacon.

MOSES OF PALERMO — Sicilian, Jew; Arabic into Latin

1. Translated, on order, of Charles of Anjou, King of Naples and Sicily, one medical work

FARAJ BEN SALIM — Sicilian, Jew; Arabic into Latin

1. *Kitab al Hawi* of Al Razi
2. Pseudo-galenic *De Medicinae expertis (On Experts in Medicine)*, from the Arabic version of Hunain ibn Ishaq
3. Ibn Jazla, *Taqwim al Abdan (Tables of the Body with Regard to Their Constitution)*
4. A treatise on surgery

Faraj was employed by Charles of Anjou to translate medical works. His main translation was *Kitab al Hawi*, the largest encyclopedia of Greco-Arabic medicine. Its importance can hardly be overestimated. Moslem dragomans probably helped him.

ALFONSO EL SABIO X — Spanish, Christian; Arabic into Spanish
Alfonso ordered translation of the following works:

1. Ptolemy, *Tetrabiblon*, together with commentary by Ali ibn Ridwan translated into Spanish by an unknown translator, and from Spanish into Latin by Aegidius de Thebaldis
2. Al Battani, *Canons*, by ibn Abi-l Rijal

3. Ibn al Haitham, *Kitab al Bari-Fi-Ahkam al Nujum* (Astrological Treatise) translated by Judah Ben Moses and Latinized by Aegidius de Thebaldis of Parma and Petrus de Regio

4. Ibn al Haitham, *Fi Haiat al Alam, (On the configuration of the world),* by Abraham of Toledo. This version was Latinized quite early under the name *Liber de mundo et coelo, de motibus planetarum, (Book on Heaven and the World and on the Motions of the Planets)*

5. A series of astronomical works in Spanish under the title *Libros del Saber de Astronomia (Books of the Science of Astronomy).* This was translated from the Arabic; it was also translated into Italian. The series are from 6 through 16 below.

6. Four books on stars derived from *Kitab al Kawakib al Thabita al Musawwar, (A Book on Stars)* by Abd al Rahman al Sufi, translated in 1256 by Judah Ben Moses and Guillen Arremon Daspa. These were edited with the help of two Jews, Judah Ben Moses and Samuel Ha-levi, and two Christians, John of Messina and John of Cremona.

7. Book on celestial globe, revised translation of *Kitab al Amal Bilkura al Fulkiya* by Qusta ibn Luqa

8. Two books on armils, essentially derived from al Zarqali, but elaborated on by Isaac ben Sid. The instrument described contained equatorial, ecliptical, and horizontal armils (rings); it could also be used to solve mechanically various mathematical problems.

9. Two books on the spherical astrolabe translated by Isaac ibn Sid

10. Two books on the plane astrolabe

11. Two books on atazir referring to the course of the planets

12. Two books of the universal plate, probably originally written by Abul-Hasan Al ibn Khalaf ibn Ghalib al Ansari of Cordova

13. *Book of the Safiha,* a translation of al Zarqali's treatise on astrology

14. Two books on the plates of the seven planets (aequatoria, or astrolabes)
15. Book of quadrants
16. Five books on clocks: (a) stone dial, (b) water clocks, (c) quicksilver clock, (d) candle clock, (e) clock of the palace of the hours; all translated by Isaac ibn Sid.
17. Book of the crosses, from the Arabic original by Ubaid Allah, the translation made by Judah Ben Moses and John Daspa
18. Book of the forms and images which are in heavens and of their virtues and power upon the terrestrial bodies, composed out of the writings of the ancient philosophers.

Alfonso El Sabio X was King of Castile and Leon from 1252 to 1284. He was brought up in an atmosphere impregnated with Moslem and Jewish influence. He had a school established for Muhammad al Riquti, who taught Christians, Moslems, and Jews. He incorporated the University of Salamanca in 1254 and in the same year established at Seville a Latin and Arabic school where Moslem physicians were the colleagues of Christian teachers. He gathered around him Jewish and Christian scholars to continue the work undertaken by his father: the translation of Arabic writings into Spanish and the transmission of Muslim knowledge to Christians. He also organized an institute for the translation of astronomical works from Arabic into Spanish.

JUDAH BEN MOSES — Spanish, Jew; Arabic into Spanish
1. Qusta ibn Luqa's treatise on the sphere
2. Abdl Rahman al Sufi, *Kitab al Kawakib (Book of the Stars)*
3. Ibn Abi-L-Rijal, *Kitab al Bari (The Function of the Stars)*
4. *Lapidary,* by Abolays.

Some of these treatises were also translated into Hebrew.
Judah Ben Moses was a physician, astronomer, and translator employed by Alfonso X.

SAMUEL HA-LEVI ABULAFIA — Jewish; Arabic into Spanish

ISAAC IBN SID — Spanish, Jew; Arabic into Spanish

Ibn Sid was the main worker under King Alfonso El Sabio.

1. Al Battani, *Canons*

ABRAHAM OF TOLEDO — Spanish, Jew; Arabic into Spanish

1. Ibn al Haitham's treatise on the configuration of the universe, later translated into Latin
2. A treatise of al Zarqali on the construction and the use of his astrolabe
3. The seventieth chapter of the Quran (*Surat al Muarij*) (Chapter of the Ascents) later translated into French

Abraham of Toledo was physician to Alfonso El Sabio as well as his translator.

DINIS — King of Portugal; had translations made of many books from Spanish, Latin, and Arabic into Portuguese.

SOLOMON IBN AYYUB — Spanish, Jew; Arabic into Hebrew

1. Maimonides, *Kitab al Faraid (The Book of Divine Commandments)*
2. Ibn Jonah, *Kitab al Tanbih (Book of Admonition, Awakening)*
3. In Jonah, *Kitab al Taswiya (Book of Correction, or Putting to Rights)*
4. Ibn Rushd, middle commentary on Aristotle's *De coelo (On Heaven)*
5. Ibn Sina, *Arjuzat*, medical poem

Ibn Ayyub was also a physician and a writer.

SHEM-TOB BEN ISAAC — Spanish, Jew; Arabic into Hebrew

1. Ibn Rushd's middle commentary on Aristotle's *De anima (On the Soul)*

2. *Kitab al Tasrif (Medicine)* of Abul Qasim al Zahrawi (1258)
3. *Kitab al Mansuri* by al Razi, a compilation of ten books based on Greek science
4. Hippocrates' *Aphorisms*

Ben Isaac, also a physician translated two important medical works, *Al Tasrif* and *Al Mansuri*. Thus Moslem medicine became available to the growing number of Jewish physicians who did not know Arabic. *Al Tasrif* was translated also into Hebrew at about the same time in France by Meshullam Ben Jonah.

ZERAHIAH GRACIAN — Spanish, Jew; Arabic into Hebrew

1. Aristotle's *Physics, Metaphysics; De coelo et mundo; De anima (On Heaven and the World; On the Soul)*
2. Themistios' commentary on *De coelo*
3. The Neoplatonic treatise *De causis et symptomatibus (On Causes and Symptoms)*
4. Al Farabi's treatise *On the Nature of the Soul*
5. Ibn Rushd's middle commentary on Aristotle's *Physics, Metaphysics,* and *De coelo*
6. The first two books of ibn Sina's *Canon*
7. Some texts of Galen which had been translated into Arabic by Hunain ibn Ishaq
8. Maimonides' aphorisms and *Jima (Philosophical and Medical Collections)*

Gracian was a philosopher and a physician. Most of his work was done in Barcelona, Toledo, and Rome for a Roman rabbi.

MOSES IBN TIBBON — 1240-1283; French, Jew; Arabic into Hebrew

His translations are so numerous that for convenience they may be divided into four groups: philosophy and theology, mathematics and astronomy, mechanics and physics, medicine.

Philosophy and Theology, Nos. 1 to 8 below, are the transla-

tions of ibn Rushd's commentaries on Aristotle. These are the
most important of his philosophical translations. All refer to the
Jami (Collections), synopsis, except 6, dealing with middle commentary, the *Talkhis*.

1. *Kitab al Asma al Tabii (Book on Hydrostatic Balance)*
2. *Kitab al Sama Wal Alam (Book on Theology)*
3. *Kitab al Kun Wal Fasad (Philosophical Synopsis)*
4. *Kitab al Athar al Ulwiyat (Book on Meteors)*
5. *Kitab al Nafs (Book on the Soul)*
6. Middle Commentary *Talkhis (On Physics)*
7. *Parva Naturalia (Small Things in Nature)*
8. *Metaphysics*
9. Themistios, commentary on Book A of the *Metaphysics*
   from the Arabic version of Ishaq ibn Hunain, revised by
   Thabit ibn Qurra
10. Al Batalyusi, *Kitab al Hadaiq*; lost in Arabic, it compares
    the world with an imaginary sphere
11. Al Farabi, *Kitab al Mabadi (Book of Origins)*, a philosophi-
    cal and political treatise
12. Maimonides, *Kitab al Saraj (Book of the Lamp)*
13. Maimonides, *Kitab al Sumum (Book of Poison)*
14. Maimonides, *Maqala Fi Sinat al Mantiq* (The Art of Logic)

Mathematics and Astronomy:

15. Euclid, *Elements*
16. Geminos on astronomy
17. Theodosios of Bithyna, *Spherics*, from the Arabic version
    by Qusta ibn Luqa
18. Jabir ibn Aflah, *Kitab al Haia (Islah al Majisti)*
19. Muhammad al Hassar, treatise on arithmetic and algebra
20. Al Bitruji, *Kitab al Haia*

Mechanics and Physics:

21. Aristotle's *Problems: Masail al Tabiyat (Questions on the
    Nature of Things)* from the Arabic version by Hunain ibn
    Ishaq

Medicine:
22. Ibn Sina, *Arjuzat* with Ibn Rushd's commentaries
23. Ibn Sina, *Al Qanun al Saghir (The Abbreviated Canon)*
24. Ibn al Jazzar, *Zad al Musafir (Traveler's Provisions)*
25. Hunain ibn Ishaq, some works on medicine
26. Al Razi, *Kitab Aqrabadhin (On Antidotary)*
27. Al Razi, *Kitab al Taqsim Wal Tashjir*, or *Taqsim al Ila (Division and Distribution of Diseases)*
28. Maimonides, *Maqala Fi Tadbir al Sihha*
29. Maimonides, *Al Sumum Wal Mutaharriz Min al Adwiya al Qitalah (On Poisons and Antidotes)*
30. Maimonides, commentary on Hippocrates *Aphorisms*

Some of the works listed here had been translated into Latin as early as the time of Constantine the African and Gerard of Cremona.

JACOB BEN MAHIR IBN TIBBON — French, Jew; Arabic into Hebrew
1. *Kitab al Kurra al Mutaharrakat (Movement of Heavenly Bodies)* by Ishaq ibn Hunain and Qusta ibn Luqa
2. Euclid, *Elements*, in fifteen books
3. Euclid, *Kitab al Mafrudat (Determined Points or Lines)*, by Ishaq ibn Hunain and Qusta ibn Luqa
4. Menelaos of Alexandria, *Spherics*, from Ishaq ibn Hunain and Qusta ibn Luqa
5. *Kitab al Amal bil Kurra al fulkiya*, or *Al-Kabir (Use of the Celestial Sphere*, or *Of the Great Sphere)*, by Qusta ibn Luqa.
6. *Fi-Haiat al Alam (On the Configuration of the World)* by ibn al Haitham.
7. *Kitab al Amal bil asturlab (Use of the Astrolabe)*, by ibn al Saffar
8. *Kitab al Amal bil Safiha al Zijiya* (Treatise on the Astrolabe)
   (The *Safiha* is a universal instrument making possible observations and reductions in regard to planets.)

9. *Balance of Speculation,* by al Ghazzali
10. *Islah al Majisti (Corrections of al Majisti)* by Jabir ibn Aflah
11. *Compendium of the Organon,* by ibn Rushd
12. *Commentary on Aristotelian Zoology,* by ibn Rushd

Tibbon was a grandson of Samuel Ben Judah ibn Tibbon, the great translator; Jacob was a mathematician, astronomer, and zoologist. Most of the Arabic texts translated into Hebrew were also translated into Latin or Spanish; some of these Hebrew versions were then translated into Latin. Out of the twelve translations, nine deal with mathematics and astronomy, two with philosophy, and one with zoology. The earliest of these translations dates from 1255 (Euclid); the latest, 1302 (ibn Rushd's *Zoology*).

JACOB IBN ABBASI — Spanish, Jew; Arabic into Hebrew

1. *Kitab al Siraj,* by Maimonides

NATHAN HAMEATI — Italian, Jew; Arabic into Hebrew

1. *Aphorisms* of Hippocrates, with Galen's commentaries
2. Ibn Sina's *Qanun*
3. *Muntakhab Fi Ilaj al Ain* (treatise on eye diseases), by Ammar ibn Ali
4. Maimonides, *Aphorisms*
5. A treatise on venesection by al Razi
6. Abu-l-Qasim's *Tasrif, (Treatise on Surgery and Obstetrics)*
7. Ibn Zuhr's *Kitab al Aghdhiya (Book of Foodstuffs)*
8. Galen's commentary upon Hippocrates' *Air, Waters, and Places,* begun by Hameati, finished by his son

Nathan was nicknamed the prince of translators, or the Italian Tibbonid (ibn Tibbon). His work was continued by his son Solomon and grandson Samuel, 1350-1400. Amar ibn Ali's *Muntakhab Fi Ilaj al Ain* was translated for the famous papal physician Maestro Gajo.

SAMUEL BEN JACOB OF CAPUA — Italian, Jew; Arabic into Hebrew

1. Treatise on purgatives and emetics by Masawaih al Maridini

AHITUB BEN ISAAC — Italian, Jew; Arabic into Hebrew

1. Maimonides' logic, *Maqala Fi Sinat al Mantiq*

NASIR AL DIN AL TUSI — is credited with some translations from Arabic into Persian.

ABU-L-FARAJ — Arabic into Syriac. He was to the Syrian world what Albertus Magnus was to the Latin.

MEKHITAR OF ANI — Arabic into Armenian

MANFRED — Sicilian, Christian; King of Sicily. The interest in Arabic and Hebrew learning shown by Frederick II was continued by Manfred (see Herman the German and Batholomew of Messina) and by his conqueror and successor, Charles of Anjou. Manfred probably himself translated into Hebrew *The Book of the Apple,* a pseudo-Aristotelian dialogue, later lost in Arabic.

JOHN OF CAPUA — Italian, Jew; Hebrew into Latin

1. *The Taisir (The Book of Simplification of Therapy and Diet)* of ibn Zuhr
2. A treatise on diet by Maimonides, *Maqala Fi Tadbir al Sihha*
3. The fables of Kalila Wa Dimna

Maimonides' *Maqala Fi Tadbir al Sihha* was translated at the request of the papal physician. It is John of Capua's version of Kalila Wa Dimna that became popular in the West as well as in the East.

PARAVICIUS — flourished in Venice, translated the Hebrew version of ibn Zuhr's *Taisir* into Latin.

ALDOBRANDIN OF SIENA — French, Christian; Latin into French

Aldobrandin wrote a medical treatise, *Le Régime du corps*; Parts 1 and 2 are derived primarily from ibn Sina and secondarily from al Razi and ali Ibn Abbas; Part 3 is an adaptation of the *Kitab al Adwiya al Mufrada Wal Aghdhiya (Introduction to Medicine)* of Ishaq al Israili, and Part 4 is translated almost verbatim from the *Kitab al Mansuri* of al Razi. He was a Tuscan physician and physician to Beatrice of Savoy. All the Arab texts were known to him only through their Latin translation. He was acquainted with the writings and translations of Hunain ibn Ishaq and Constantine the African. His treatise is the first monument of French medical literature, and one of the first of French scientific literature.

DAVID CASLARI — French, Jew; Latin into Hebrew

1. Some of Galen's work which had been translated from the Arabic into Latin by Gerard of Cremona

SOLOMON BEN MELGUEIL — French, Jew; Latin into Hebrew

1. Anonymous commentary on Aristotle's *De Somno et vigilia (On Sleep and Wakefulness)*
2. Ibn Sina: Summary of Aristotle's *De coelo et mundo (On Heaven and the World)*
3. Platearius, *Circa Instans (On the Present)*
4. Some of ibn Rushd's metaphysics

Raymond Lull, the Catalan scholar, did not actually translate any Arabic works by others but deserves recognition here because of his lifelong efforts to promote Arabic studies. Lull was a philosopher, missionary, and a great Arabic scholar. He wrote mostly in Catalan and many of his writings were immediately translated into Latin. Lull wrote several books in Arabic which he later translated into Catalan, Latin, or both. For example, *Liber Contemplationis in Deum,* or *The Book of Contemplations of God,* was translated into Catalan and Latin. It is an encyclopedia of practical theology, including satirical descriptions of such various classes of people as physicians, lawyers, and teachers; algebraical symbols and geometrical figures are used to represent thoughts or to abbreviate their expression. This encyclopedia runs to nearly a million words.

Another book written in Arabic and translated into Latin by Lull was *Liber de Gentili* (*Book of the Gentile*) in which he has a Jew, a Christian, and a Moslem expound in turn the superiority of their faith. Lull believed that Jews and Moslems could be converted to Christianity by peaceful methods. It appears also that Lull in his *Compendium Logicae Algazelis* (*Compendium of the Logic of al Ghazzali*) first made a summary of al Ghazzali's logic in Arabic and then translated it into Latin in 1290. A poem of his in Catalan on the one hundred names of God was obviously inspired by the Moslem writings on the ninety names of God.

Lull, one of the main channels through which Moslem lore was transmitted to the Christian West, was also the founder of Western Orientalism. In his zeal to convert Jews and Moslems, he realized the need of schools by which missionaries could obtain practical knowledge of Arabic and Hebrew. The Arabic college of Miramar in Majorca was founded at Lull's request by James II, and Pope John XXI in 1276. Another school of Arabic was established in Valencia and a school of Arabic and Hebrew in Xatvia in the closing years of the thirteenth century. At his insistence, and because of his petition to the Council of Vienna, that council established five schools for missionaries—a normal one at the Roman curia, and four others, Bologna, Paris, Oxford, and Salamanca—where three languages would be taught, Hebrew, Chaldean and Arabic.

What was happening in this century is clear. Western writers from all over Europe (Christians and Jews) were absorbing Greco-Arabic knowledge.

FIRST HALF OF THE FOURTEENTH CENTURY

STEPHEN SON OF ARNOLD — Spanish, Christian; Arabic into Latin

1. *Kitab al Amal bil—Kurra al Fulkiya (The Book on the Use of the Spherical Astrolabe)*, by Qusta ibn Luqa
2. *Fi Tadbir al Abdan (On the Care of the Body)*, by Qusta ibn Luqa
3. *Viridarium, id est Espositio antidotarii Nicolai Salernitani (The Garden, that is, an Exposition of the Antidotes of Nicholas of Salerno)*
4. *Experimenta (Experiments)*
5. *De evacuatione (On Evacuation)*
6. *De febribus (On Fevers)*
7. *Prognosticationes (Prognostications)*
8. *Regimen contra defectum coitus (Guide Against Failure in Coitus)*
9. A treatise on cataract
10. *Defensarium vitae (Preservative of Life)*, ascribed to Arnold of Villanova
11. A treatise on bloodletting
12. *Annotationes in Anatomiam Mundini (Annotations on the Anatomy of Mundinus)*
13. *Isagoge in Hippocratis et Galeni Physiologiae partem anatomicam (Introduction to the Anatomy of Hippocrates and Galen)*

JUDAH BONSENYOR — French, Jew; Arabic into Catalan

1. A collection of Arabic proverbs together with ibn Gabirol's *Mukhtar al Jawahir (The Improvement of Moral Qualities)*

MOSES BEN SOLOMON OF BEAUCAIRE — French, Jew; teacher of Qalonymos ben Qalonymos, philosopher and translator; Arabic into Hebrew

1. Ibn Rushd's *Tafsir (Commentary)* on Aristotle's *Metaphysics*

SAMSON BEN SOLOMON — Jewish translator; Arabic into Hebrew

1. *Sixteen Books of Galen.* This is the name given to the Byzantine Canon of Galenic writings. These Canons and Hippocratic Canons form the core of Arabic medicine.

QALONYMOS BEN DAVID THE ELDER — French, Jew; Arabic into Hebrew

1. *Tahafut al Tahafut (Incoherence of Incoherence)*, Ibn Rushd's treatise against al Ghazzali's *Incoherence of Philosophy*

QALONYMOS BEN QALONYMOS — French, Jew; Arabic into Hebrew

1. Archimedes, treatise on the sphere and the cylinder, from the Arabic version by Qusta ibn Luqa.
2. Archimedes, treatise translated by Thabit ibn Qurra into Hebrew and into Latin by Gerard of Cremona
3. Apollonios, extracts from the Geometry
4. Hypsicles, Book XIV of Euclid's *Elements* together with commentaries
5. Nicomachos of Gerasa, some of his work together with a summary by Abu Sulaiman Rabi ibn Yahya
6. Ptolemy's Geography
7. Some of Ptolemy's work *(Centiloquium)* translated from the Greek by Ahmad ibn Yusuf al Misri and into Hebrew under the title *Sefer Ha-peri ha-niqra meah dibburim*
8. Galen, several works, some translated from the Greek by Hunain ibn Ishaq
9. Eutocios, commentary on Archimedes
10. Jabir ibn Haiyan, fragments of thesis on poison
11. Al Kindi's short treatise on nativities
12. Al Kindi's work on the causes, in the higher spheres, which determine rain
13. Al Kindi's treatise on dampness and rain
14. Thabit ibn Qurra, *Kitab Fi Shakl al Qatta (On Anatomy)*

15. Hunain ibn Ishaq, *Kitab al Madkhal Fil Tibb* (*Introduction to Medicine*)
16. Al Farabi, *Kitab Fil Aql Wal Maqul* (*On the Intellect*)
17. Al Farabi, *Kitab Ihsa al Ulum* (*Enumeration of the Sciences*). This work had been translated into Latin by Domingo Gundisalvo and Gerard of Cremona.
18. Al Farabi, *Kitab Fima Yanbaghi An Yuqaddama Qabla Talim al Falsafat* (*On Philosophical Propaedeutics*)
19. Ikhwan al Safa, treatise in which various kinds of animals are compared with man
20. Ali ibn Ridwan, *Kitab al Umud Fi Usul al Tibb* (*Principles of Medicine*)
21. *Ibn al Samh,* treatise on cylinders and cones
22. Jabir ibn Aflah, extracts from the *Islah al Majisti*
23. *Analytica,* extracts concerning Chapter 16 of Book I
24. Ibn Rushd's *Sharh* or *Tafsir* (*Long Commentary*)
25. Ibn Rushd's *Talkhis* (*Intermediate Commentary*)
26. Ibn Rushd's *Jami* (*Collections*); the *Tafsir, Talkhis,* and *Jami* are commentaries on Aristotle's work.
27. Abu Sadan, treatise on the triangle
28. Ibn Rushd's *Tahafut al Tahafut,* translated from Hebrew into Latin

Qalonymos's translations of ibn Rushd's commentaries are definite and important links in the transmission of ibn Rushd's works to the West.

SAMUEL BEN JUDAH OF MARSEILLE — Arabic into Hebrew

1. Ibn Rushd's commentary on Plato's *Republic*
2. Ibn Rushd's *Jami* (*Collections*) dealing with Aristotle's *Organon*
3. Aristotle's *Organon,* translation of questions concerning obscure points in ibn Rushd's commentary
4. Aristotle's *Ethics,* translation of ibn Rushd's *Talkhis* (*Intermediate Commentary*) on the *Nicomachean Ethics*

5. Hypsicles, supplement to *Book XIV of Euclid's Elements*
6. Ptolemy, ibn Rushd's commentary on parts I-III of the *Almagest*
7. Alexander of Aphrodisias, Book I of the treatise on the soul, translated into Arabic by Ishaq ibn Hunain
8. Abu Abdallah Muhammad ibn Muadh of Seville, treatise on the total solar eclipse that occurred in 1079
9. Treatise on dawn by ibn Muadh
10. Al Zarqali, treatise on the movement of fixed stars
11. Jabir ibn Aflah, *Islah al Majisti*
12. Ibn Rushd's commentaries on Plato, Aristotle, and Ptolemy

TODROS TODROSI — French, Jew; Arabic into Hebrew

1. Al Farabi, *Kitab Uyun al Masail (Sources of the Questions)*, including sixty theses concerning Aristotelianism
2. Ibn Sina, *Kitab al Najat (Salvation)*, a summary of Aristotelian philosophy
3. Ibn Rushd, translation of the *Talkhis* on Aristotle's *Rhetoric*
4. Ibn Rushd, translation of the *Talkhis* on the *Poetics.*
5. Ibn Rushd, three dissertations, the first two dealing with ibn Sina's theory of the three modes of being, the third with prescience
6. Ibn Rushd, fragment of the treatise on the material intellect including the views of Empedocles, Pythagoras, and Plato on the soul

SOLOMON BONIRAC — Italian, Jew; Arabic into Hebrew

1. Some of Galen's work put into Arabic from the Greek by Hunain ibn Ishaq

SOLOMON BEN PATER — Castilian, Jew; Arabic into Hebrew

1. *Kitab Fi Haiat al Alam (On the Form of the Universe)*, by ibn al Haitham

ISAAC BEN NATHAN OF CORDOVA — Spanish, Jew; Arabic into Hebrew

1. Al Ghazzali, treatise on questions answered by al Ghazzali
2. Maimonides, *Maqala Fil-Tawhid (On the Unity of God)*
3. Joseph Ben Judah ibn Aqnin, treatise on the necessary existence and how things proceed from it
4. Muhammad Ibn Muhammad al Tabrizi, commentary on Maimonides' introduction to the second part of the *Dalalat al Hairin (Guide for the Perplexed)*

SAMUEL BEN SOLOMON HAMEATI — Italian, Jew; Arabic into Hebrew

1. Galen's commentary on Hippocrates' regimen in acute diseases, from the Arabic version, *Tafsir il Kitab Tadbir al Amrad al Hadda*, by Hunain ibn Ishaq, *(Book on the Care of Acute Diseases)*
2. Ibn Zuhr's medical works *(Lamp of Healing)*

Ben Solomon Hameati was the last of a great family of Jewish-Italian translators from Arabic into Hebrew

SALAMA — Egyptian theologian, translated some parts of the Bible from Arabic into Ethiopian

PIETRO D'ABANO — Italian philosopher, astrologer, physician; Greek and French into Latin

Greek into Latin:

1. *Problemata* of Aristotle *(Problems or Propositions)*
2. *Problemata,* ascribed to Alexander of Aphrodisias
3. *Problemata* of Cassios the Iatrosophist
4. Completed the translation of the fourteenth book of Galen's *Methodus, etc. (Methods, etc.); De optima nostri corporis compositione (On the Best Composition of Our Body); De cholera nigra (On Black Cholera); De sectis (On Classes); De ingenio sanitatis (On the Nature of Health)*

French into Latin:

1. Abraham Ben Ezra's astrological treatise; this French version had before him been Latinized by Henry Bate.

NICCOLÒ DA REGGIO — Italian, Christian; Greek into Latin

Galenic writings:

1. *De victu attenuante (On Inadequate Diet)*
2. *De utilitate particularum (On the Usefulness of Small Parts)*
3. *De passionibus uniuscuisque particulae (On the Illnesses of Each Small Part)*
4. *Subfiguratio empirica (Empirical Shaping)*
5. *De optima doctrinatione (On the Best Learning)*
6. *De partibus artis medicativae (On the Parts of the Art of Medicine)*
7. *De constitutione artis medicativae (On the Basis for the Art of Medicine)*
8. *De sequela operationum animae (On the Consequence of the Operations of the Soul)*
9. *De consuetudinibus (On Customs)*
10. *De causis procatarcticis (On Causes of Diagnosis)*
11. *De tumoribus praeter naturam (On Unnatural Tumors)*
12. *De typo (Concerning Type)*
13. *De comate secundum hippocratem (On Coma According to Hippocrates)*
14. *Liber prognosticorum (Book of Prognostication)*
15. *De virtute simplicis medicinae (On the Value of Simple Medicine)*
16. *De phlebotomia (On Bleeding)*
17. *De sanguisucis (On Leeches)*
18. *De facile acquisibilibus (On Remedies Easily Obtained)*
19. *De usu partium corporis humani (On the Use of the Parts of the Human Body)*, his main work

20. *De causis continentibus libellus (Small Book on Associated Sicknesses)*
21. *De sectis ad eos qui introducuntur (On Classes for Beginners)*
22. *De optima secta ad thrasybulum (On the Best Class for Thrasybulus)*
23. *De morborum temporibus (On the Times of Diseases)*
24. *De totius morbi temporibus (On the Times of the Whole Disease)*

Probably also:

> *De anatomia oculorum (On the Anatomy of the Eyes); De virtutibus centaureae (On the Values of Centaury); De gyneciis (On Female Conditions); An omnes particulae animalis quod foetatur fiant simul (Whether All the Little Parts of an Animal Decay Simultaneously)*

Works probably by Galen:

25. *De utilitate respirationis (On the Usefulness of Breathing)*
26. *De sanitate tuenda (On Guarding Health)*
27. *De temporibus utilibus egentis (On Useful Times for the Needy)*
28. *Hippocratis aphorismi cum commento Galeni (Aphorisms of Hippocrates with Galen's Commentary)*
29. *De febribus ad glaucomam (On Fevers with Glaucoma)*
30. *De introductione medicorum (On the Preparation of Physicians)*
31. *De substantia virtutum naturalium (On the Substance of Natural Qualities)*
32. *Liber de regimine acutorum (Book on the Care of Those in Danger)*
33. *De virtute consuetudinis (On the Value of Habit)*

Da Reggio was a physician as well as a translator of medical, especially anatomical works. He translated for Charles II of Anjou, King of Naples, who, like other Angevin kings, was interested in promoting Greek knowledge. Later Niccolò was under the patronage of Robert, King of Naples, and other notables. King Robert obtained Greek manuscripts for Niccolò from Emperor Andronicos II and had Niccolò translate them. Niccolò was the first to reveal Greek medicine without Moslem alterations. His translation of Galen's treatise on the use of the parts of the body is a landmark in the history of anatomy and medicine.

JUDAH BEN MOSES BEN DANIEL — Italian, Jew; Latin into Hebrew

1. Pseudo-Aristotelian *De causis* (*On Diseases*), probably translated not from the Arabic, but from the version made by Gerard of Cremona. A similar translation was made from the Arabic at an earlier time.
2. Boetius, *De uno et unitate* (*On the One and Unity*)
3. Ibn Rushd, *De substantia orbis* (*On the substance of the world*), probably from the version ascribed to Michael Scot
4. Thomas Aquinas, *De ideologia* (*On Ideology*)
5. Also other short texts by Aquinas, Albertus Magnus, and Giles of Rome

SAMUEL BENVENISTE — Spanish, Jew; Latin into Hebrew

1. Boetius, *De consolatione philosophiae* (*On Consolation of Philosophy*)
2. Maimonides' treatise on asthma

DAVID BEN YOM-TOB BEN BILA — Portuguese, Jew; Latin into Hebrew

1. Salus Vitae, dealing with the twelve medical or magical virtues of pulverized snake skin; derived from an Arabic or Egyptian original
2. Treatise on logic

PROUVILLE — French, Christian; Latin into French

1. Surgical treatise of Abbé Poutrel

PIERRE DE PARIS

1. *Politics* of Aristotle
2. *The Psalms*
3. *Consolatio philosophiae (Consolation of Philosophy) of* Boetius

ARNOLD OF QUINQUEMPOIX — French, Christian; Latin into French

1. Some work from Abraham Ben Meir ibn Ezra
2. Abu Masshar's astrological works
3. Some of al Kindi's works
4. *Book of Redemption*
5. Treatise on astrology, *Liber Hermetis (Book of Hermes)*

BERSUIRE — French, Christian; Latin into French

1. Livy's *Decades,* (History of Rome) at the request of King John the Good

Bersuire was a friend of Petrarch. He was in difficulties on several occasions because he did not hide his opinion that the Church was corrupt and needed reforms. The translation of Livy's *Decades* into French was very successful and of great importance for the revival of ancient literature and for the blossoming of the Renaissance in France.

NICOLAS DE LA HORBE — French, Christian; Latin into French

1. *Liber astronomicus* by Guido Bonatti, who had based his astrology on Arabic sources, especially on al Farghani

VIGNAI — French, Christian; Latin into French

At least twelve sizeable translations from the Latin, for John the Good, Duke of Normandy

BARTHOLOMEW OF BOLOGNA and JACOB THE DRAGOMAN, Latin into Armenian

ROBERT MANNING and MICHAEL OF NORTHGATE also translated from French into English. Their work is significant for the history of the English language.

BENCIVENNI — Italian, Christian

Translator of Arabic writings of al Farghani and al Razi, from French into Italian.

There were also translations from Sanskrit into Persian, Telugu, and Chinese, and from Tibetan into Mongolian.

During the fourteenth century there was a gradual decline in translations from Arabic into Latin. By the end of the century they had almost ceased. The translations from Arabic into Latin had been the first to come and they were the first to go.

The predominance of Arabic into Latin translations was replaced by Arabic into Hebrew translations, a situation even more pronounced in the last half of the century.

Translations of Greek into Latin revived in the last half of the thirteenth century and continued into the first half of the fourteenth.

Also of considerable importance were the translations from Latin into Hebrew and Latin into French. At the beginning of the fourteenth century the main classics of Greek and Arabic medicine were available to the Latin reader. The number of books available in Hebrew was much smaller. As Western Jews had lost their Arabic contacts, more translations from Arabic into Hebrew became necessary for them.

There were many other translations made from one language to another. By count, there are over thirty combinations.

SECOND HALF OF THE FOURTEENTH CENTURY

JOSEPH BEN JOSHUA I HA-LORQI — Spanish, Jew; Arabic into Hebrew

1. Revision of previous Hebrew translations of Maimonide's treatise on the art of logic

JOSEPH BEN JOSHUA II HA-LORQI — Spanish, Jew; Arabic into Hebrew

1. Part of Qanun of ibn Sina and revision of other works of ibn Sina

DAVID IBN YAISH — Spanish, Jew; Arabic into Hebrew

1. Arabic version of the Greek treatise on domestic economy. This treatise is lost in Greek, but extant in Arabic, Hebrew, and Latin; through these versions, especially the Arabic, it exerted some influence upon medieval thought.

JUDAH BEN SOLOMON NATHAN — French, Jew; Arabic and Latin into Hebrew

1. Umaiya Ibn Abi-L-Salt, *Kitab al Adwiya al Mufrada;* this had been translated earlier into Latin by Arnold of Villanova
2. Al Ghazzali, *Maqasid al Falsifa (The Goals of Philosophers)*
3. Ibn Wafid: *Kitab al Wisad (Book of the Pillow)*
4. *De vino,* by Arnold of Villanova (treatise on wines and their medical uses)
5. Treatise on fevers

For preparation of his *Maqasid al Falsifa,* Judah used *Kitab al Shifa (Philosophical Encyclopedia)* and *Kitab al Najat (Salvation)* of ibn Sina; *Kitab al Mabahith al Sharqiya (Book on the Contributions of the East)* by Fakhr al Din al Razi; and ibn Rushd's *Tahafut al Tahafut.* John of Seville had translated this work into Latin earlier, as had Isaac of Albalag. For the preparation of *Kitab al Wisad,* Judah used the Arabic works of ibn Sina and the Latin writings of Gilbert the Englishman and John St. Amand.

JACOB CARSONO — Spanish, Jew; Arabic and Latin into Hebrew

1. His own Arabic writings into Hebrew

SAMUEL IBN MOTOT — Castilian, Jew

1. Abdallah ibn Muhammad al Batalyusi, *Kitab al Hadaiq (The Orchard)*, lost in Arabic, but known in Hebrew by the translation of Moses ibn Tibbon
2. Abraham Ben David Ha-Levi, *Kitab al Aqidah al Rafiah (The Sublime Faith)*, a philosophical treatise.
3. Pseudo-Abraham Ben Ezra, *Book of Substance*, dealing with astrology

SOLOMON BEN LABI — French; Jew; Arabic into Hebrew

1. *Kitab al Aqidah al Rafiah (The Sublime Faith)*

JUDAH BEN SOLOMON IBN LABI — Jewish financier, patron of learning, who flourished in Saragossa. He patronized the works of at least three Jewish scholars:

1. Meir Alguadez translated the *Nicomachean Ethics* from Latin into Hebrew.
2. Zerahiah Ben Isaac Ha-Levi (called Saladin) translated *Kitab Tahafut al Falasifa* of al Ghazzali from Arabic into Hebrew.
3. Joshua Ben Joseph Lorqi II compiled an Arabic treatise on the powers and qualities of various foods and of simple and composite drugs. This treatise is lost in Arabic, but extant in Hebrew.

SOLOMON BEN ELIJAH — Greek, Jew; Greek and Arabic into Hebrew

1. Treatise on the astrolabe ascribed to Ptolemy

MOSES OF ROQUEMAURE — Spanish, Jew; Latin into Hebrew

1. He translated the *Lilium medicinae (The Bud or Sprout of Health)*, of Bernard of Gordon dealing with hygiene, physiology, psychology, morality, topography and also the medical climatology of Seville.

LEON JOSEPH OF CARCASSONNE — Spanish, Jew; Latin into Hebrew

1. Commentary on al Razi's work
2. Gerald de Solo, *Introductorium juvenum, sive de regimine corporis humani* (*Introduction to the Training of Youth, or on the Care of the Human Body*)
3. Jean de Tournemire, *Treatise on urine*
4. Jean de Tournemire, *Clarification of the ninth book* (*Kitab al Mansuri by al Razi*)
5. Pseudo-Hippocratic works; an Arabic treatise on astrology

Leon Joseph emphasized the need of better medical books in Hebrew, since the available translations from the Arabic and the Latin were insufficient. He scored the insufficiency of the translation of ibn Sina's *Qanun* by Nathan Ha-Meati as revised by Lorqi and others. Leon had great difficulty obtaining medical books for translation, for the Montpellier doctors had threatened to anathematize anyone selling such books to Jews.

JEKUTHIEL BEN SOLOMON — Spanish, Jew; Latin into Hebrew

1. *Lilium medicinae (Lily of Medicine)* of Bernard of Gordon

ABRAHAM ABIGDOR — French, Jew; Latin into Hebrew

1. Ibn Sina's *Qanun,* that part of it dealing with recipes as translated earlier by Bernard Alberti of Montpellier
2. Some medical works by Arnold of Villanova
3. Gerald de Solo's *Introduction to the Young*
4. *Almanzori,* abridged translation of the ninth book of the *Kitab al Mansuri* of al Razi, from the Latin by Gerard of Cremona
5. *Higgaion (Meditation)* by Peter of Spain
6. Commentary on ibn Rushd's *Talkhis*

In his original works Abraham used al Ghazzali's *Maqasid al Falasifa,* translated earlier by John of Seville into Hebrew; he also refers to al Farabi, Maimonides, and ibn Rushd.

SOLOMON ABIGDOR — Spanish, Jew; Latin into Hebrew

1. *Methods of Judgment*
2. The *Appearance of the Wheels;* an allusion to Ezekiel's vision in the Bible.

SOLOMON BEN NATHAN CRESCAS — Spanish, Jew; Latin into Hebrew

1. Book of Apollonuis of Tyana

SOLOMON BEN DAVID DAVIN — Spanish, Jew; Latin into Hebrew

1. The astronomical tables of Paris
2. Ibn Abi-L-Rijal, *Kitab al Bari, (The Function of the Stars)* translated earlier from the Arabic into Spanish and from Spanish into Latin

BENJAMIN BEN ISAAC OF CARCASSONNE — Spanish, Jew; Latin into Hebrew

1. Treatise on the corruption of the air and the plague

JACOB BEN JUDAH CABRET — Catalan, Jew; Latin into Hebrew

1. Treatise on medical astrology by Arnold of Villanova

MEIR ALGUADEZ — Spanish, Jew; Latin into Hebrew

1. Aristotle's *Ethics*

SHEMTOB SHAPRUT — Spanish, Jew; Latin into Hebrew

1. Parts of the four Gospels, including all of Matthew

PROCHOROS CYDONES — Salonican, Christian; Latin into Greek

1. St. Jerome's preface to the Vulgate (IV)
2. Various writings of St. Augustine

3. Books I and II of the *De differentiis topicis (On Topical Differences)* of Boetius (VI-I)
4. Three texts of St. Thomas Aquinas; eighty-two articles taken from the third part of *Summa theologica (Theological Summa)*

DEMETRIOS CYDONES — Salonican, Christian; Latin into Greek

1. Mass of Ambrosian rite
2. Writings of St. Augustine
3. Fulgentius
4. St. Anselm
5. *Summa contra Gentiles,* St. Thomas Aquinas

Demetrios Cydones was one of the first translators from Latin into Greek and one of the first interpreters of Roman Catholic theology to the Eastern Orthodox theologians.

JEAN DE SY — French, Christian; Latin into French

1. French translation of the Bible

MARTIN DE SAINT-GILLES — French, Christian; Latin into French

1. Aphorisms of Hippocrates with Galen's commentary

JOHN CORBECHON, FOULUCHAT, PRESLES, JEAN DANDIN, HESDIN EUDES, JACQUES BOUCHANT, EVARD DE CONTY, and GOELIN: they were all Christians and translators, mostly of religious works, from Latin into French. With the exception of Eudes, all flourished under Charles V (the Wise) of France, who encouraged and subsidized them in their translations. The most notable of these translators is Goelin.

TREVISA — English, Christian; Latin into English

1. *Polychronicon* (A universal chronicle from the beginning of the world to the fourteenth century written by Ranaulf Higden)

2. The Gospel of Nicodemos
3. Other religious writings

LEONZIO PILATO — Greek, Christian; Greek into Latin

1. Homer's *Iliad*. Petrarch persuaded him to translate the *Iliad* and acquainted him with Boccaccio, who obtained a position for Leonzio for the first time to teach Greek in Florence.

NICOLE ORESME — French, Christian; Latin into French

Noted not only for his translations of Aristotle and Ptolemy but also for his original treatises, which embody ideas traceable to the writings of ibn Sina, al Ghazzali, and others.

JOANNES JACOBI — Spanish, Christian; Arabic into Catalan
Various works

JOHN OF YPRES — French, Christian; Latin into French

Many travel accounts; he was one of the earliest scholars to appreciate the significance of geographical discoveries.

During the last half of the fourteenth century, Latin into Hebrew translations predominated. Latin had thus finally arrived, in that translations were made not only into it, but out of it, and in large quantities.

Arabic was being translated into Hebrew, Catalan, and Latin. The Arabic into Latin translation, once a mighty stream, had just about dried up. The translations into Catalan were also slight relative to the translations from Arabic into Hebrew. The translations from Arabic into Hebrew were second largest, surpassed only by translations from Latin into Hebrew.

CHAPTER EIGHT

Translations and the Rise of Western Civilization: Conclusions

We have seen that the twelfth century, and to a lesser extent the thirteenth, was essentially a period of transition, absorption, and fusion. The youngest of the three leading cultures of the time, Islam, had begun to decline. The transition was accomplished almost entirely by translation of Arabic writings into Latin and Hebrew. The fusion that took place resulted from the closeness and interaction of the Christian and Moslem cultures. The exchange of cultural activities between Europe and the Arab world, between Christians, Jews, and Moslems, was never more intense than during this era.

By the middle of the thirteenth century, there had finally developed in Western Europe the core of a new civilization, a core essentially Greco-Arabic-Latin. By the end of the thirteenth century, the genius of Western Christendom had begun to take the cultural lead. Since then, that genius has largely been the creator of modern culture.

We saw earlier how the bulk of Greek science was gradually translated into Arabic. At the beginning of the twelfth century, Greek knowledge was available in Greek and in Arabic, but was more accessible in the latter form. Moreover, many Greek works were lost in the original but available in Arabic translations. When the West became sufficiently mature to feel the need for

132

deeper knowledge, when it wanted to renew its contacts with ancient thought, it turned to Arabic sources.

Thus, the main intellectual task of the twelfth and thirteenth centuries was one of translation. Much of the intellectual energy of medieval times was spent not in the creation of new intellectual values but in the transmission of older ones. Knowledge was won not by fresh and independent investigation but by translation, chiefly from Arabic.

A rough examination of the translators and their work leads to the conclusion that while works were translated from Greek into Latin, from Arabic into Hebrew, from Hebrew into Latin, from Latin into French, and so on, the translations from Arabic into Latin were far more important than all the others.

These translations occurred in three waves. The first wave is represented by Constantine the African in the second half of the eleventh century, the second by John of Seville in the first half of the twelfth; the third wave of Arabic knowledge washing over the West resulted from the great work of Gerard of Cremona in the second half of the twelfth century.

The most important channel by which the new learning reached Western Europe was the Spanish peninsula. Spain, however was not the only route. Africa, through Constantine the African; England through Adelard of Bath; various cities in the Byzantine empire; and the island of Sicily, where the Arabs had ruled from 902 to 1091; all share in the honor.

Translations were well planned and organized and occupied the active years of many great minds. Some were "ordered" by rulers for a specific purpose; others were made at the behest of churchmen or government officials. The bulk of the translations, however, were made because of the thirst for new knowledge and the desire of Latindom to lead in culture and science. By the end of the fourteenth century, there was little of real importance in the Arabic scientific literature which scholars had not made accessible to the Europeans.

The cultural importance of the work of Islamic scholars and

translators for the development of science and humanities can hardly be overestimated. At the same time, this translation work propelled the Arabs to cultural prominence during the Middle Ages. Nothing else was more instrumental in their spectacular rise. Their military victories were impressive, but they produced nothing but fear and submission, qualities not conducive to progress or cultural achievements. The Arab world had remained in a culturally obscure position until it discovered the works of the Greeks. Realizing that unearthing and transmitting these works would bring them a long way toward establishing their own culture, they made the most of this opportunity.

Similarly, when the Western world realized its need of knowledge to compete with Islam on equal terms and to fulfill its own aspirations, it turned to translation again to transfer Greco-Arabic knowlege into Latin and other languages.

Arab ascendancy then was initiated and carried on by translation; we have seen that the Latin West and Europe in general turned to the same means to lift themselves to cultural prominence. Thus, the roots of Western thought are a mixture of Greco-Arabic and Hebrew thought. The blending of an East-West body of knowledge gained strength from each of its sources.

SELECTED BIBLIOGRAPHY

AQUINAS, Saint Thomas, *Summa Contra Gentiles*, trans. by the English Dominican Fathers. London: Burns, Oates and Washbourne, Ltd., 1924.

—, *Summa Theologica*, trans. by the English Dominican Province, rev. ed. London: Burns, Oates and Washbourne, Ltd., 1911.

ARBERRY, A. J., *Avicenna on Theology*. London: John Murray, 1951.

—, *The Spiritual Physick of Rhazes*. London: John Murray, 1950.

ARISTOTLE, *Organon, or Logical Treatises with the Introduction of Porphyry*, trans. by Octavius F. Owen, Vols. I and II. London: Henry G. Bohn, 1853.

ARNOLD, Sir Thomas, and Alfred Guillaume, *Legacy of Islam*. New York: Oxford University Press, 1931.

BERGH, Van Den, Simon, *Averroes' Tahafut al-Tahafut (The Incoherence of Incoherence)*. Vols. I and II. London: Oxford University Press, 1954.

DANTE Alighieri, *The Divine Comedy*, Carlyle-Wicksteed translation. New York: Modern Library, 1950.

DAVINCI, Leonardo, *The Notebook*, ed. and trans. by Edward MacCurdy. New York: George Braziller, 1955.

Encyclopedia of Islam, 4 vols. and supplement. Leiden, Netherlands: E. J. Brill, Ltd., 1913.

FARABI, Al, *Al Majmu (The Collections)*, Muhammad Badr al Din, Cairo, 1907.

FARABI, Al, *The Fusul Al-Madani of Al Farabi (The Aphorisms of the Statesman)*, trans. by D. M. Dunlop. London: Cambridge University Press, 1961.

FARMER, H. G., *The Arabian Influence on Musical Theory*. London: Luzac & Co., 1925.

——, *History of Arabian Music to the XIIIth Century*. London: Luzac & Co., 1929.

FARRUKH, Omar A., *The Arab Genius in Science and Philosophy*, trans. by John B. Hardie. Washington, D. C.: American Council of Learned Societies, 1954.

GHAZZALI, Al, *Ayyuha'l-Walad (My Boy)*, Arabic text, French translation by Toufic Sabbagh. Beirut, Lebanon: International Commission for the Translation of Masterpieces, 1951.

GUILLAUME, Alfred, *Islam*. Baltimore, Md.: Penguin Books, 1954.

HAMMOND, Robert, *The Philosophy of Al Farabi and Its Influence on Medieval Thought*. New York: Hobson Press, 1947.

HASKINS, Charles Homer, *Studies in Medieval Culture*. Oxford: The Clarendon Press, 1929.

HITTI, Philip K., and others, *The Arab Heritage*. Princeton, N. J.: Princeton University Press, 1944.

——, *History of the Arabs*, 6th ed. London: MacMillan and Co., Ltd., 1958.

——, *History of Syria*. New York: Macmillan and Co., Ltd., 1951.

IKHWAN AL-SAFA, *Rasail (Brothers of Sincerity)*, ed. by Khayr-al Din al Zirikli. Cairo: Al-Maktabah al Tijariyah, 1928.

ISIS, An International Review Devoted to the History of Science and Cultural Influence, official journal of the History of Science Society, published quarterly by the Johns Hopkins Press, Baltimore, Md.

ISSAWI, Charles, *An Arab Philosophy of History*. London: John Murray, 1950.

The Jewish Encyclopedia, 12 vols. New York: Funk & Wagnalls Co., 1906.

Journal of Royal Asiatic Society of Great Britain and Ireland, a review devoted to Asia and the Middle East, published semi-annually by the Society, 56 Queen Anne St., London, England.

KHALDUN, Ibn, *The Muqaddimah (An Introduction to History)*, vols. I-III, trans. by Franz Rosenthal. New York: Pantheon Books, 1958.

——, *The Muqaddama.* Maktabat al Madrasat wa Dar al Kitab al Libnani, Beirut, Lebanon, 1961.

KHALLIKAN, Ibn, *Kitab Wafayat al Ayan wa-abna al Zaman (The Deaths of Great Personages and History of Leading People of the Time),* 6 vols., Cairo: Maktabah al Nahdah al Musriyah, 1948-1950.

KROPOTKIN, Pëtr, *Mutual Aid.* Middlesex, England: Penguin Books, 1939.

LANDAU, Rom, *The Philosophy of Ibn Arabi.* New York: The Macmillan Co., 1959.

LEWIS, Bernard, *The Arabs in History,* 2nd ed. London: Hutchinson's University Library, 1956.

MAARRI, Abu al-Ala al, *Risalat al Ghufran (Treatise on Forgiveness),* ed. by Kamil Kilani. Cairo: Al Maktabah al-Tijariyah, 1923.

MACDONALD, Duncan B., *Development of Muslim Theology, Jurisprudence, and Constitutional Theory.* New York: Charles Scribner's Sons, 1903.

MAHDI, Muhsin, *Ibn Khaldun's Philosophy of History.* London: G. Allen and Unwin, 1957.

MOORE, G. F., *History of Religion.* New York: Charles Scribner's Sons, 1913.

NADIM, Ibn al, *Fihrist al Ulum (Index of All Branches of Knowledge),* ed. by G. Flügel. Leipzig: Vogel, 1871-1872.

NICHOLSON, R. A. *Literary History of the Arabs.* London: T. Fisher Unwin, 1907.

NIZAM, Al Mulk, *The Siyasat-nama or Siyar al Muluk (The Book of Government or Rules For Kings),* trans. by Hubert Darke. New Haven, Conn.: Yale University Press, 1960.

O'LEARY, DeLacy E., *Arabic Thought and Its Place in History,* New York: E. P. Dutton & Co. Inc., 1939.

——, *Arabic Thought and Its Place in History,* rev. ed. New York: Humanities Press, 1957.

——, *How Greek Science Passed to the Arabs.* London: Routledge and Kegan Paul, 1949.

PALACIOS, Miguel Asim, *Islam and the Divine Comedy*, trans. by Harold Sunderland. London: John Murray, 1926.

ROSENTHAL, Franz. *A History of Muslim Historiography*. Leiden: Netherlands, E. J. Brill, 1952.

SARTON, George, *Introduction to the History of Science*, Vols. I–III. Baltimore, Md.: Williams and Wilkins, 1927-1948.

SPENGLER, Oswald, *The Decline of the West*, Vols. I and II, trans. by Charles Francis Atkinson. New York: Alfred A. Knopf, 1926-1928.

TOYNBEE, Arnold J., *A Study of History*, Vols. I–X. London: Oxford University Press, 1955.

TOYNBEE, Paget, *Dante Studies and Research*. London: Methuen and Co., 1902.

WATT, Montgomery W., *The Faith and Practice of al Ghazzali*. London: Allen and Unwin, 1953.

INDEX OF AUTHORS AND TRANSLATORS

INDEX OF TITLES